Portobello Road

Textbook 2

Verlag Moritz Diesterweg
Frankfurt am Main

Portobello Road

Herausgegeben von Christoph Edelhoff
Erarbeitet von Ingrid Gebhard, Pat Jüngst,
Claudia Straeter-Lietz und Jürgen Wrobel
sowie Otfried Börner, Viola Kessling, Phil
Mothershaw-Rogalla, Huub Rutten,
Frank van Ruyssevelt und John H. Williams
Fachliche Beratung: Michael Blöß und Gisela
Schultz-Steinbach

Illustrationen: Steffen Gumpert, Hildesheim
Gestaltung: Creativ Design, Hildesheim
Umschlaggestaltung: Boros, Wuppertal
Vokabelanhang: Wißner Verlag, Augsburg
    Redaktion: Dr. Hildegard Kuester
    Satz: Sabine Schalwig

Zusatzmaterialien zum vorliegenden Schülerbuch

- Workbook (Best.-Nr. 3-507-71512-0)
- Kassette zum Schülerbuch (Best.-Nr. 3-507-71532-5), identischer Inhalt wie CD
- CD zum Schülerbuch (Best.-Nr. 3-507-71562-7), identischer Inhalt wie Kassette
- Teacher´s Manual (Best.-Nr. 3-507-71522-8)
- Folien (Best.-Nr. 3-507-71552-X)
- Multimedia Sprachtrainer

Gedruckt auf Papier,
das nicht mit Chlor
gebleicht wurde.
Bei der Produktion
entstehen keine
chlorkohlenwasserstoff-
haltigen Abwässer.

CHLORFREI

ISBN 3-507-71502-3

© 1999 Schroedel Verlag GmbH, Hannover

Das Werk ist in Teilen auf der Grundlage
einer Lizenz des Verlages L. C. G. Malmberg B. V.,
's-Hertogenbosch, NL, entwickelt.

Druck A ⁵ ⁴ ³ ² ¹ / Jahr 2003 2002 2001 2000 1999

Alle Drucke der Serie A sind im Unterricht parallel verwendbar,
da bis auf die Behebung von Druckfehlern untereinander
unverändert. Die letzte Zahl bezeichnet das Jahr dieses Druckes.

Reproduktionen: Köhler & Lippmann GmbH, Braunschweig
Druck: Neef + Stumme GmbH & Co. KG. Wittingen
Bindearbeiten: Langelüddecke GmbH, Braunschweig
Printed in Germany

Inhalt

Symbolerklärungen:

 Partnerarbeit

 Dieser Text ist auf CD oder Kassette.

 Gruppenarbeit

 Hierzu gibt es eine Erklärung im LiF-Teil.

Tipp oder Hilfe

Klassenprojekt

Hierzu gibt es noch
eine Übung im
Workbook.

Als Portfolio legst du dir einen
Ordner an. Hier sammelst du alles,
was du während des Schuljahres
selbst anfertigst.

Last year in Portobello Road

Back to Portobello Road!

Gillian Collins
– 12, Notting Hill
– lives with her mother
– has a cat: Fuzzy
– likes music, chocolate, make-up, clothes, and earrings
– likes to make breakfast (sometimes)
– plays football in Holland Park girls' team

Charlie Macintosh
– 12, Hendon
– his family is from the West Indies
– his aunt and uncle live in Germany
– has two sisters, Josephine and Sharon
– can run very fast, plays football, is a super goalkeeper
– is president of the Hendon Goldfish Club
– likes balloon adventures, dinosaurs, and Lisa Naumann

Vera Gulbenkian
– 12, moved from Hendon to Notting Hill in the summer holidays
– calls her parents Dan and Janet
– her dad does the cooking at home
– likes elephants, books, music, and earrings
– plays football

David Williams
– 12, Hendon
– is Gillian's cousin
– his Aunt Fay and Uncle Morgan live in Wales
– has a dog: Kenny
– works in his parents' supermarket
– likes comics and castles

Susan Johnson
– 12, Notting Hill
– has a little sister, Rita, and an older brother, Jack
– loves animals, has a dog, a hamster, and three goldfish
– likes music and popcorn
– can run fast

Karim Khan
– 13, Notting Hill
– his family is from Bombay, India
– has a sister, Sheree
– likes music and computers
– plays the guitar

After the holidays

CD

A1 Back in Notting Hill

LiF → 1, 5, 7

David: What are these? Holiday postcards? Let me see.
Vera: No, that's a photo. My dad is playing football in the park. He's not very good.
David: And the dog? Is it playing, too?
Vera: Not really. It's just running after the ball.
Charlie: Here's David's postcard from Wales. Is this where your father comes from?
David: No, my uncle lives there. Here's another photo. People are waiting for the train that goes up Snowdon. And look at this photo. We're just coming out of Caernarfon Castle.
Vera: What about you, Charlie?
Charlie: Well, I was at a pony camp for two weeks. I looked after the ponies and cleaned the stables.
Susan: Don't forget me. I stayed at home. But I had a good time. I visited a lot of friends.

Workbook
A1

Mount Snowdon

A2 David, Susan and Charlie talk about their holidays.

a) Put these words where they belong.

a lot of friends   good time   at home   Wales   Caernarfon Castle

pony camp   train   ponies   stables   uncle   Snowdon

DAVID	CHARLIE	SUSAN

b) Use your notes to speak and write about the friends' holidays.

… was (in/at) …
There was …
… had/stayed/visited/cleaned/looked after …

Example: David was in Wales.

Workbook A2, A3

Land und Leute Die Britischen Inseln

Die Karte hinten im Buch zeigt die Britischen Inseln, *the British Isles*. Sie bestehen aus den beiden großen Inseln Großbritannien *(Great Britain)* und Irland *(Ireland)* sowie einer Reihe kleinerer Inseln wie z.B. *Jersey, Isle of Man* oder den *Shetland Islands*.
Großbritannien selbst besteht auch wieder aus drei Teilen: England, Schottland und Wales. Kannst du ihre Hauptstädte herausfinden?

England ist der größte Teil, aber Menschen aus Schottland oder Wales können sehr ärgerlich werden, wenn ihr sie als Engländer bezeichnet. Sie sind alle Briten und haben eine gemeinsame Königin. Aber jeder Landesteil ist sehr stolz auf seine eigene Geschichte und Tradition.

Wales liegt westlich von England. Es ist nicht größer als Hessen. Ein Drittel der Bevölkerung spricht walisisch *(Welsh)*, aber alle sprechen auch englisch. Walisisch ist sehr schwer zu lesen, wie z.B. der lange Ortsname auf dem Foto unten links.

Schottland liegt nördlich von England. Zu Schottland gehören für viele Leute Schottenröcke, Dudelsäcke, karge Landschaft, hohe Berge, schöne Seen und Burgen. Sehr bekannt sind das Ungeheuer von Loch Ness, das Musikfestival in Edinburgh und die schottischen Wettkämpfe *(Highland Games)*.

Llanfair… Railway Station, Wales

Durdle Door, Dorset, England

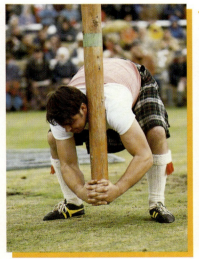

Highland Games, Scotland

Urquhart Castle, Loch Ness, Scotland

A3   Here are some sentences from A1.

My dad is playing football. My uncle lives there. I was at a pony camp.
I cleaned the stables. The train goes up Snowdon. I looked after the ponies.
I had a good time. People are waiting for the train. I stayed at home.
The dog is just running after the ball. I visited a lot of friends.

Can you write lists like this?

simple present: My uncle lives there. …

simple past: I was at …

present progressive: My dad is playing …

LiF → 1, 5

Workbook → A4

A4 Look at these postcards. They are from pupils from Holland Park School.

1

Hi friends!
Great place here,
not too much rain.
Saw the Loch Ness
monster. It looked
like Mr Graham.
Love,
Brenda Tan Fong

2

3

Lovely weather.
Lovely beach.
Lovely food.
Lovely water.
Lovely apartment.
Lovely people.
Allaha ısmarladık,
Emma

So this is America.
Everything really big. Big hamburgers,
big buildings. Yesterday I walked up
the Statue of Liberty and went on
a boat trip around Manhattan.
See you soon,
Pete

We're here in Vienna.
Saw all the bones in
Stephansdom - exciting.
Weather fantastic, dry
and sunny. People are
really friendly. My
German is very good
now.
Bye for now,
Geoff Pattison

4

a) Brenda was in …
That's postcard number …
Pete was …
Geoff …
Emma …
Mary …

b) Find as much information as you can:

5

Hello everyone!
Stayed near this lovely
old castle on our way
to the south of
Germany.
Met a really nice boy,
Mark. He is so good-looking,
dark hair, tall …
Love from
Mary

Countries	Turkey	Scotland	USA	Germany	Austria
Sights	beach				
Weather	…				
Other information	lovely …				
Postcard from	…				

CD

LiF → 6

portfolio

tip

A5 Brighton Summer Festival

a) Listen to the radio report from the Summer Festival
at the seaside town of Brighton in England.

b) What do you know?

The reporter		lying in the sun.
Claire and Tom		landing in the water.
A band	is	playing music.
A big red balloon		swimming in the sea.
Mr Graham		talking from the beach in Brighton.
A lot of people	are	collecting empty drink cans.
Some people		enjoying the festival.
		looking for somewhere to land.
		talking to a reporter.

A6 It's good to have nice weather in your holidays. What about YOUR holidays?

At first … then … later … at the end of the holidays …

it was	hot warm cold	dry sunny windy cloudy rainy wet foggy

we had	some a lot of no	rain / sun / wind / clouds / fog

In deinem Portfolio
sammelst du alles,
was du während des
Schuljahres selbst
anfertigst.

Workbook
A5 – A7

B 1 Look at the pictures in B2.
What do you think – is the text about

– Charlie's favourite pony?
– a trip to the beach?
– a pony race on the last day?
– a riding lesson?

CD

LiF → 2, 8

B 2 Charlie's last day at the pony camp

Charlie had a lot of fun at the pony camp. He enjoyed the race on the last day. Charlie wasn't in the race – he was the commentator.

"… and here we are, campers, on a cloudy but warm Saturday morning. My name is Charlie, Charlie Macintosh, and I'm your commentator today for this big race. We have five ponies and five really good riders – and they're off! Patsy Mulloy on Flame is in front – oh dear, Sunflower is hungry – she's stopping in front of some flowers – oh no, Rhonda Smith is out of the race.

Flame is still in front and now Terry Dixon on Sugar Boy is coming and – wait a minute – now it's Prince and Dark Crystal. They're both jumping the hedge and they're leaving the racecourse! That's not what Wally Simpson and Yoyo Conroy want! They're out of the race, too. Well, it's only Flame and Sugar Boy now. And Sugar Boy is stopping! What is he doing now? He's turning around! Oh no!

That only leaves Flame – and here's Patsy Mulloy on Flame at the finishing line. Well done, Patsy! And Flame! This year's Pony Camp Race winner!"

B 3 Find the names of the five ponies and of their riders in the text.

Example:

 Patsy rode ...

B 4 The race

What do you think: "TRUE", "FALSE" or "DON'T KNOW"?

1 Charlie enjoyed the race.
2 There were six ponies in the race.
3 Terry Dixon rode Dark Crystal.
4 Rhonda Smith rode Sunflower.
5 Sunflower stopped and looked at sunflowers.
6 Prince jumped the hedge.
7 Sugar Boy was a very young pony.
8 Terry Dixon had a lot of fun at the race.
9 Four ponies crossed the finishing line.
10 Patsy Mulloy was the winner on Flame.
11 Prince and Dark Crystal left the racecourse.
12 Flame turned around.

LiF → 1

B 5

a) Find the simple past forms of these verbs in B4:

| be | ride | cross | enjoy | stop |
| have | jump | turn around | leave | look at |

b) Put the pairs in two lists. Which verbs are easy/difficult for you?

easy	difficult
...	...
...	...

Workbook ➤ B1, B2

21

B 6 Talk about YOUR holidays.

Work in groups of four.
Take notes of the answers you get.

	went to	my grandmother/aunt/… Cologne/…
I	stayed	at home.

Where did you go for your holidays?

Where did you stay?

In	a hotel.
	a holiday apartment.
On	a camp site.
With	some friends.
	my aunt/…

How long did you stay there?

It was	great!
	not bad.
	terrible.
We had a lot of/some …

One day/week/…
Two days/weeks.
Three …

What was the weather like?
food
water
hotel

What did you do?

I	went	swimming.
We		cycling.
	watched	…
	visited	…
	…	…

This shows you how to take notes.

Markus:
Italy
camp site
two weeks
hot and sunny
swimming
beach ball

B 7 My holidays

I went to Spain for my holidays.
We stayed in an apartment in
Alicante. We went swimming
every day. It was very hot!
I met a girl from Scotland
and we played beach ball together.

I stayed at home.
It was good fun.
The weather was great.
I went swimming and
met some friends.
I stayed in bed until
11 o'clock every morning.
One day I went on a
boat trip on the Rhine.

What can you write about YOUR holidays?
You can use B6 and B7 for help.

C1 Back at school

Vera lives in Notting Hill now and goes to Holland Park School. This is her second day at the new school. She is sitting next to her friend Gillian in the science lesson. She is writing a letter to Victor. She met him in Brighton in the summer holidays.

82 Westbourne Terrace
London W2 4HH

Dear Victor,

Thanks a million for your letter. Here I am back at school. Wish I was in Brighton again. Oh, it was great. Why can't we have longer holidays? I'm now in the same class as my friend Gillian - we moved to Notting Hill last month. Don't forget my new address. It's at the top of this letter.

I'm writing this in the science lesson. Our teacher is busy and he can't see me. I hate science. It smells.

Love your photo - your T-shirt is great. I'm thinking about the fun we had in Brighton and can't wait - oops, Mr Hartley is looking at me

Workbook → C1

1

tip

For theme 2 you need more information about London. Write to:
London Tourist Board
Glen House
Stag Place
London SW1E 5LT
Great Britain.
Look at WB C1 for help.

Land und Leute Britische Adressen

Kannst du Unterschiede zwischen einer britischen und einer deutschen Anschrift finden? Straßenbezeichnungen werden bei britischen Adressen oft abgekürzt, z.B. *Rd* für *Road*, *St* für *Street* und *Ter* für *Terrace*. Übrigens, die Postleitzahl (hier W2 4HH) heißt *postcode* auf Englisch.

Vera Gulbenkian
82 Westbourne Terrace
London W2 4HH

C2 Which of these things can Vera see in the classroom?

board calculator mouse maps teacher pencil
chairs Bunsen burners pupils ruler pens
schoolbags door smoke eraser envelope book
water sandwiches magazine

She can see …
There is a … There are …
There is/are no …

C3 a) Now make a list of things in YOUR classroom today.

How many round / square /… things can you find?

round

square

red

soft

hard

brown

b) Where are YOU and your friends sitting in your English lesson today?
Use these words:

at the back   at the front   in the middle
on the left/right   behind   in front of   next to   …

Example: Vera is sitting next to Gillian.
Vera and Gillian are sitting in the middle.

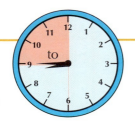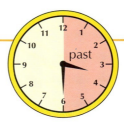

C4

Vera and Gillian's school day starts at quarter to nine and ends at half past three. Lunch break is from quarter past one to half past two.

Find a partner and talk about YOUR school day.
Ask the questions and answer them.

> – When does school start?
> – When does it end?
> – When are the breaks?
> – Which subjects do you have today? When?
> – How many lessons do you have every day?
> – Which are your favourite subjects this year?
> – Which subjects don't you like?
> – What is new this year?
> – Do you think the breaks are long enough?
>   … the lessons are too short?
>   … school starts too late?
>   … school ends too early?

pair work

Workbook ➤ **C2 – C6**

CD

C5   The school chant   © Printha Ellis

It's another Monday.
Not a number one day!

Felt tips, paper clips,
Eraser, ballpoint, glue.
Textbooks, workbooks,
Exercise books, too.

      Do you have my pen?
      I can't find it again!

It's another Monday.
Not a number one day!

Calculator, ruler,
Sandwich for the break.
Now my bag is full of
All the things I take!

      Do you have my pencil case?
      It's never in the right place!

It's another Monday.
Not a number one day!

C6 Your school

You want to introduce YOUR school to a partner class in Great Britain.
Make
– a video or
– a photo presentation or
– a collage or
– a cassette.

You can
– talk/write about how many pupils, teachers, … there are.
– show/describe the school building, the classrooms, the gym, …
– show/interview the headteacher, the school secretary, the caretaker, …
– present a class, …
– present an open day at YOUR school.

Work in groups.
Plan what you want to do.
Your teacher can help you.

Around London

A1 Imagine a tiger – which of these words go with tiger?

lovely   exciting   friendly   pets   sleepy

cage   Asia   clever   Africa   yellow with black stripes

cat   zoo   hungry   small

dangerous   fast   wild   big   interesting   slow

Write a list and use the words to speak about tigers.

Tigers live in …   Tigers are (always/sometimes/…) …
Tigers can be …   Tigers have …

CD

A2 Catch the tiger!

LiF → 7, 8

Gillian is at home alone. Her mother is visiting some friends. Gillian is listening to the news on the radio. There is a tiger walking in the streets of London! Gillian is <u>not</u> happy – she is very frightened.

Newsreader: … and the police are looking for it now. The keeper went to the cage at five thirty and the tiger wasn't there. It's somewhere in the streets of London …

Gillian: Help! Perhaps it's in our street. Is it walking outside our house? Where's Mum?

Newsreader: The zoo is in Regent's Park. The tiger is always sleepy after its meal and it ate at three o'clock. Is it sleeping in someone's garden?

Gillian: Here? In London? Oooh, what's that noise?

Mrs Collins: Oh, hello, Gillian? What's the matter?

A3 - A5 ← Workbook

Gillian: Oh, Mum, quick. Close the door! They're looking for a tiger from the zoo. It's in our street.

Newsreader: Here's the latest news. The tiger is in Kensington Gardens, near the Round Pond. The police and the keepers are trying to catch it now. It's very sleepy …

Gillian: Oh, thank goodness!

Add new words to your list.
Speak about the tiger in the street.
You can start like this:
The police are looking for a tiger.
The tiger wasn't in its …

A3 Lunch for the animals

a) Work with a partner. What do these animals eat?

pair work

> Yes, they do. /
> I think they do.

hamsters – meat
horses – mice
elephants – fish
sea lions – plants
crocodiles – grass
snakes – carrots

> Do hamsters eat meat?

> I don't think
> they do. I think
> they eat …

> No, they don't. They eat …

LiF → 9

b) Find more animals and speak about their food.

A4 Animal quiz

a) Do you know the answers?

1 What is black and white and very frightened?

2 What do polar bears have for lunch?

3 How do you get four elephants into a small car?

b) What can you see here?

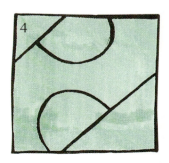

Answers on p. 31.

A5 The animals' holidays

Look at the pictures. What do the animals usually do and what are they doing now?
Example:
The tiger usually … (live / in the zoo) but tonight it is walking in the streets.
The tiger usually lives in the zoo but tonight it is walking in the streets.

1 The mice usually stay in their holes but now they are … (dance / on the table)

2 The fish usually swims in the aquarium but today it is … (swim / in the sea)

3 The chimpanzee usually … (play / in its cage) but today it is eating in a snack bar.

4 The dog usually sleeps outside but tonight it is … (sleep / in the bed)

5 The cat usually … (catch / mice) but today it is going to the supermarket.

6 The rabbit usually stays in the fields but today … (fly / to Mexico)

LiF → 5

Workbook
A3 – A5

A6 My favourite animals

Dolphins
Clever, friendly
Swimming, jumping, singing
They are more peaceful than people
Dolphins

tip

You can make your own poem. Look at your workbook, A6.

Answers to
Animal quiz on page 29:
1 A cow on a bike.
2 Iceburgers.
3 Two in the back and two in the front.
4 A giraffe in front of a mirror.
5 A cat going up a tree.
6 Someone with a dog.

Workbook
➤ A6, A7

B1 Meeting friends

Charlie's uncle and aunt from Germany are in London for a week. Their German friends, Mr and Mrs Naumann and their daughter Lisa, are with them. Charlie wants to show Lisa the sights of London. They take the tube to Oxford Circus to meet Gillian and Karim.

Karim: Well, he's late. He said half past two and now it's twenty-nine minutes to three.

Gillian: Oh, come on, Karim. There he is. Look!

Karim: Wow! Who's the beautiful girl with him?

Charlie: Hi! Sorry we're late. This is Lisa. Lisa, this is Karim and this is Gillian.

Lisa: Hello, Gillian. Hello, Karim.

Gillian: Hi, Lisa. Where are you from?

Lisa: I'm from Germany.

Charlie: Yeah, my aunt and uncle are here from Germany and Lisa's parents came with them. So I'm showing Lisa the sights.

Karim: Lisa, you're lucky. A tiger was walking in the streets of London yesterday. It's really good that Charlie is with you.

Lisa: A tiger? Oh no.

Gillian: Yes, I was so frightened. It ran away from the zoo. Later they found it in Kensington Gardens. You know, I have an idea! Why don't we all go to the zoo? I want to see the tiger in its cage – just to be sure ...

Karim: Great idea. Let's take the tube and ...

CD

B2

a) Can you add the names here?

… are in London for a week.
… are with them.
… is Mr and Mrs Naumann's daughter.
… wants to show Lisa the sights of London.
… are waiting for Charlie.
… thinks Lisa is beautiful.
… tells Lisa about the tiger.
… wants to see the tiger in its cage.
… go to the zoo.

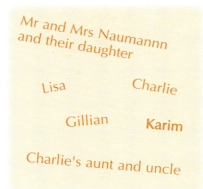

Mr and Mrs Naumannn
and their daughter

Lisa   Charlie

Gillian   Karim

Charlie's aunt and uncle

**b) What can you find out about Lisa? Look at the text and the picture in B1.
Work with a partner and write your sentences down.**

pair work

Workbook B1

B3 Animals at the zoo

CROCODILES
South America
sharp teeth
meat, fish
2.30pm feeding time

POLAR BEARS
North Pole
white fur
fish, meat
3.30pm feeding time

ELEPHANTS
1994/95 • Africa
tusks and trunk
plants
3.45pm bath time

CHIMPANZEE
1992 • Africa
long arms
plants, fruit, eggs
4pm feeding time

FLAMINGOS
North America
long pink legs
plants, fish
2pm feeding time

LION
1996 • Africa
light brown fur
meat
3.15pm feeding time

HIPPOPOTAMUS
1980 • Africa
big mouth
plants
5pm feeding time

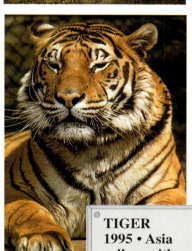

SEA LIONS
Europe
flippers
fish
2.45pm feeding time

TIGER
1995 • Asia
yellow with
black stripes
meat
3pm feeding time

a) What do you know about these animals? Write texts.

The … come/s from …   It has / They have …   It is / They are …
       Feeding time is at …   … eat/s …

Workbook
→ B2–B5

b) Which animals do YOU want to see? Say why.

I want to see the … because it is / they are …

funny   wild   dangerous   noisy   exciting
interesting   very big/small   lovely   cuddly

portfolio

tip

**c) Is there a zoo near your home? When did you last go there?
What did you see?**

I went to the zoo last …. I saw …. It was / They were …

Use a dictionary for
more animal names.

B4

Tiger

I'm a tiger
Striped with fur
Don't come near
Or I might[1] Grrr
Don't come near
Or I might growl[2]
Don't come near
Or I might
BITE!

© Mary Ann Hoberman

My name is Supermouse

My name is Supermouse
I live in a Superhouse
I do as I please[7]
I eat Supercheese
I chase Superrats
And I frighten nine lives
Out of all Supercats.[8]

© John Kitching

Dogs

Dogs big, dogs small
Dogs short, dogs tall
Dogs fat, dogs thin
Dogs that make a dreadful[3] din[4]

Dogs smooth,[5] dogs hairy
Dogs friendly, dogs scary[6]
Dogs brown, dogs white
Dogs that bark all through the night

Dogs that run, dogs that walk
Dogs that make you think they'll talk
Dogs awake, dogs asleep
Dogs for the blind, dogs for the sheep

The best of all the dogs I know
goes with me everywhere I go.

© John Kitching

Geraldine Giraffe

The longest
ever
woolly
scarf
was
worn
by
Geraldine
Giraffe.
Around
her
neck
the
scarf
she
wound,[9]
but
it
still
trailed[10]
upon[11]
the
ground.

© Colin West

Listen to all the poems. Choose your favourite poem and learn it.

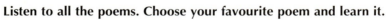

[1] might [maɪt] *könnte* [2] growl [graʊl] *knurren* [3] dreadful ['dredfʊl] *schrecklich*
[4] din [dɪn] *Lärm* [5] smooth [smuːð] *glatt* [6] scary ['skɛərɪ] *beängstigend* [7] I do as I please
Ich tu, was mir gefällt [8] I frighten nine lives out of all Supercats *Ich erschrecke alle Superkatzen zu Tode*
[9] wind [waɪnd], wound [waʊnd] *wickeln, wickelte* [10] trail [treɪl] *schleifen* [11] upon [ə'pɒn] *auf*

B5 London Zoo

LONDON ZOO ™

CONSERVATION IN ACTION

When London Zoo first opened in 1827 it was not like a modern zoo. The animals had cages like the houses in their home countries. There were grass huts for African animals, for example. Many of the 12,000 animals today were born in zoos. They do not know Africa or Asia or America or the North Pole.

Other animals are very rare and not many live outside zoos: the giant panda, for example, or the tigers, the hippos and the Asian lions.

A zoo always has money problems. You can adopt an animal at London Zoo for a year. For £20 you can adopt a guinea pig, a hamster, a mouse or a rabbit, a gecko or a small snake. You can also share bigger animals with other people: the food for a giraffe is £1,500, for a tiger it's £3,000, and for an elephant £6,000.

In one day, an elephant can eat a lot of hay, carrots, cabbages, apples, potatoes, bread and salt – all washed down with 100 litres of water.

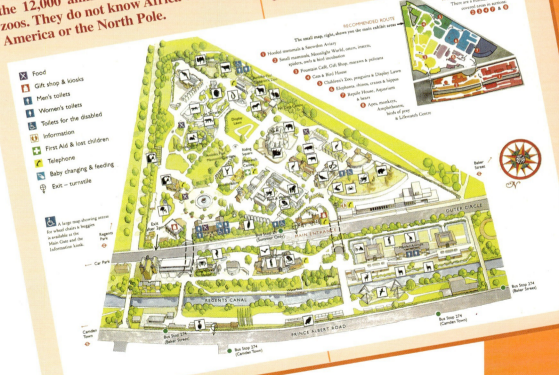

Find out from the text:

places:
Africa

rare animals:

LONDON ZOO

animals' food:

animals to adopt:

Workbook → B6

37

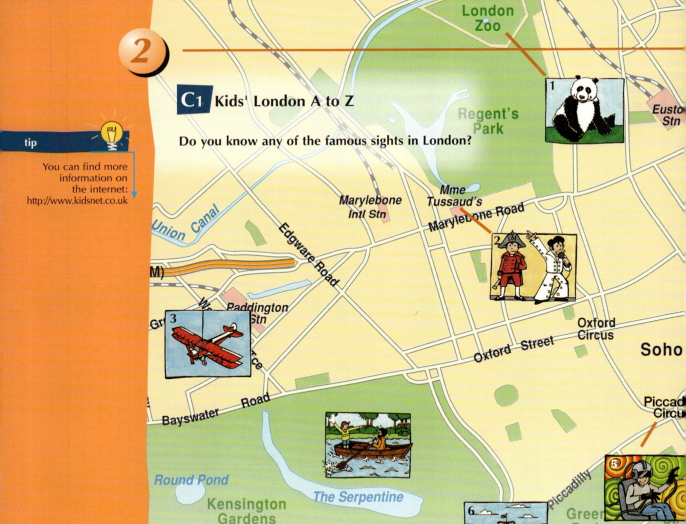

C1 Kids' London A to Z

Do you know any of the famous sights in London?

Buckingham Palace
You want to drink tea with the Queen? No chance! But visit some of her rooms in August or September.

Covent Garden
Shops and stalls, toys and music, jugglers and clowns – you can find them all at Covent Garden. Enjoy an exciting afternoon, have an ice-cream and watch, watch, watch!

Hyde Park
Londoners and tourists come here to relax, sit in a boat, enjoy the sun or listen to one of the speakers at Speaker's Corner on Sunday morning.

London Toy and Model Museum
The place for fans of toys and models – model trains, ships and planes but also modern Japanese toys, dolls and teddy bears.
Open: 10am – 5.30pm

London Transport Museum
Get on a double-decker bus, set the signals for a train, ride a locomotive.
Open: 10am – 6pm

Madame Tussaud's
Meet the famous people of the world – in wax. Kings, queens, pop stars, sportspersons – even Jack the Ripper is waiting for you.
Open: 9am – 5.30pm

King's Cross Stn

Pancras Stn

a Museum

City of London

Liverpool Street Stn

8

St. Paul's Cathedral

10

Cannon Street Stn

Tower

Charing Cross Stn

Waterloo Bridge

River Thames

London Bridge

Royal National Theatre

London Bridge Stn

Tower Bridge

Whitehall

West-minster Bridge

Waterloo Intl Stn

Southwark

Houses of Parliament

Science Museum

Science means adventure: ride a snowboard, look at the stars, fly to the moon …
Open: 10am – 6pm

Segaworld

The first European cyberspace entertainment park. Video games, computer games and more video games and more computer games …
Open: 10am – midnight

Tower Bridge

This famous bridge is next to the Tower of London. It opens up when large ships are passing.

The Tower of London

Castle with several towers. Come and see the cannons and the uniforms of the past.
Open: Mon to Sat, 9am – 6pm

The Zoo

The bears are back! And with them there are elephants, snakes, tree snails, spiders and sharks and about 12,000 more animals for you to look at.
Open: 10am – 5.30pm

Elephant Castle Stn

Workbook → C1, C2

Land und Leute The Tower of London

Der Tower ist eine riesige Burganlage mit mehreren Türmen. Der normannische König Wilhelm der Eroberer ließ sie im Jahr 1078 erbauen. Der Tower wurde unter anderem als Gefängnis genutzt. Eine ganze Reihe berühmter Menschen wurde dort hingerichtet.
Zur Zeit Heinrichs III (1207 – 1272) gab es im Tower eine Art Tiergarten, zu dem auch ein Eisbär gehörte. Er durfte – an einer langen Leine – in der Themse fischen.

Heute ist der Tower ein Museum, unter anderem für Waffen und Rüstungen aus der englischen Geschichte. Etwa 4 Millionen Besucher besichtigen jedes Jahr den Tower. Die längste Schlange gibt es in dem Teil, in dem die Kronjuwelen zu bewundern sind:
z.B. der Rubin des Schwarzen Prinzen, einer der größten Diamanten der Erde (der Koh-i-noor) und die Krone, die die Queen bei offiziellen Anlässen trägt (mit 3.000 Diamanten, Rubinen, Saphiren und Perlen).
Eine weitere Besonderheit des Tower sind die Wächter, die Beefeater. Diesen Spitznamen bekamen sie vermutlich, weil sie immer besonders gut genährt aussahen. Sie tragen noch heute die gleichen Uniformen wie im Jahre 1500.

C2

a) **Look at the map in C1. Can you find all the places?**

I think picture number ... must be / is ...

b) **Now work with a partner and ask and answer.**

Where can you go	when it is sunny? when it is rainy? when you have no money?	
and see	clowns, video games, animals, trains, ships, toys, uniforms, buses, jugglers, dolls, cannons, castles, famous people	?

C3 Imagine YOU have one day in London.
Choose three places. Write down what you can do and see there.
You can use the texts in C1 for help.

portfolio

> My day in London
>
> First I want to see …
> There I can …
> I think it's interesting to …

CD

C4 **Where did Lisa go?**

Lisa spent a day with Charlie and his friends. She visited four places.

Listen to the CD and find out where she went.

I think she went to … first.
Then she was at …
Afterwards she saw …
Later she went … and …

Workbook ➤ C3 – C5

C5 A guided tour in YOUR town

Work in small groups, not more than four people.
Draw pictures or find photos of interesting places in YOUR town.
Make a brochure and write short texts about the places you can visit.
Show your brochure to your class. Compare the brochures.

… is in the … of Germany.
… people live in our town.
You can visit …
In the evening …
Many visitors like …
Young people in our town can …

Over to you

CD

A1 The big hero

David always reads a lot of comics.
Then he dreams: "What will I be when I grow up?"

When he reads westerns, he wants to be a cowboy in the Wild West. "I'll ride my beautiful horse and go on long treks with the cattle from Mexico to Colorado. I'll have riding lessons first, of course."

When he reads science fiction comics, he wants to be an astronaut. "I'll fly to the moon, of course, and then I'll fly to Mars. Perhaps I'll be the first man on Jupiter or Mars …"

Sometimes he reads comics about heroes from the past.
"Robin Hood! That was a great time! Bows and arrows. Yes! I'll ask Mum and Dad for a bow and arrow for my birthday. Mmm, good idea. Bow and arrow – then I'll be a sportsman in the next Olympics and I'll ride my horse and I'll win the race …"

Workbook
A1 ←

A2

a) Find the words for David's dreams and write them down.

a cowboy	an astronaut	a sportsman
ride a horse	fly …	ask …
go …	fly …	be …
have …	be …	win …

Or perhaps he'll be a/an …

LiF → 10

b) Talk about your notes:

David thinks he'll be a …
Then he'll …
And he'll …

c) And you? What will YOU be when you are old enough?

pilot   stuntman   boxer   filmstar

vet

Example: Perhaps I'll be a vet .   stewardess   singer   …

Workbook
A2 – A4

Land und Leute   Robin Hood

Viele Geschichten werden über die Abenteuer von Robin Hood erzählt. Es gibt Lieder, Romane und Filme über ihn.

Robin Hoods echter Name soll Robert Earl of Huntingdon gewesen sein. Er lebte im 12. Jahrhundert und war ein Untertan von König Richard Löwenherz. Als der König das Land für einige Zeit verließ, regierte sein Bruder Prinz John. Der wollte reicher werden und nahm den Anhängern von Richard Löwenherz das Land weg. Da sammelte Robin Hood eine Gruppe von Freunden um sich. Sie wollten den Verrätern den Reichtum wieder wegnehmen, um ihn den Armen zu schenken.

Bald waren Robin Hood und seine Freunde berühmt und jeder erkannte sie an ihren grünen Jacken und ihren Pfeilen und Bogen. Sie lebten gemeinsam in einem Wald namens Sherwood Forest bei Nottingham.

Noch heute steht der Name Robin Hood für Gerechtigkeit und Mut.

A3

a) Match the types of stories and the names.

1 westerns	a Robin Hood
2 science fiction stories	b Old Shatterhand
3 adventure stories	c Superman
4 fairy tales	d Snow White
5 horror stories	e Hansel and Gretel
6 cartoons	f Frankenstein
	g Major Kira
	…

b) Choose the type of story you like best.
Find a name that goes with it.
Write down as much as you can about it.
Here is some help for you:

My favourite stories are … . My favourite person is …

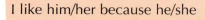

He/she	is …
	lives in …
	has …
	helps …
	can …

I like him/her because he/she	wants to …	
	is	strong.
		beautiful.
		clever.
		interesting.
		funny.

tip

Use your dictionary
for more words.

portfolio

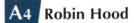

A4 Robin Hood

A5, A6 ◄— **Workbook**

A5 Robin Hood or Little Red Riding Hood?

You know about Robin Hood now. Do you know the fairy tale of Little Red Riding Hood?

a) Look at these words. Which words go with Robin Hood? Which go with Little Red Riding Hood?
Work with a partner and write the words in two lists.

pair work

little girl   forest   hat   clever   big nose

old woman

sheriff   put on   hang   grandmother

big mouth

mother   cake

big eyes   catch   wolf

kill   glasses   eat

in bed   ride

bow and arrow   horse   oak tree   green clothes

b) Use the words in your Robin Hood list.
Write a text about Robin Hood.

portfolio

Workbook A7

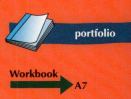

CD

B1 Ready, steady, go!

Quizmaster: And now the Roaring Tigers! OK, now you have 30 seconds. How many words can you find on the topic "Winter"? Ready, steady, go!
Max: Er, snow.
Claire: Ice.
Max: Er, ice-skating.
Claire: Snowman.
Max: Uhm, snowboard.
Claire: Gloves.
Max: Uhm, cold.
Claire: Hat.
Max: Scarf.
Claire: Boots.

Max: Pullover!
Claire: Socks.
Max: Warm woolly vests!
Quizmaster: Stop! Time's up, Roaring Tigers. Thirteen points. Well done, Claire and Max!
Claire and Max: Thanks.
Quizmaster: Now over to you – the Old Shoes.

teamwork

B2 Try and play the game "Ready, steady, go!"
You need a quizmaster and two teams.
Find exciting names for the teams first.
You need a stopwatch – 30 seconds for one topic.
Draw a grid on the board and write down the points.

Workbook
B1

Topic	Dream Team	Champions
		++++ ++++ I
zoo	++++ I	++++ ++++
music	++++ ++++ III	
holidays	++++ ++++ ++++ I	++++ ++++ II
school		

B3 The winners

HENDON SCHOOL HERALD

Max and Claire are in year 8 at our school. Max is very tall and slim and he wears glasses. He is very shy. He speaks very slowly because he is always thinking. He is very good at information technology and at history. Claire is not tall but she is very slim, too. She likes reading and surfing the internet. But she is also quite shy. She is not so good at sports.

This year Max and Claire are the stars of the school. Together they are the Roaring Tigers, Hendon School's best team for the TV show "Ready, steady, go!" When Max plays the game, he answers very quickly. Claire looks beautiful under the lights. Everyone wants to know them now. Their parents are very proud. But Max and Claire say, "We're just a very good team."

3

B4

a) What can you say about Claire and Max?

Claire	Max

is ... likes ... wears ... is (not) good at ... speaks ...

b) What are YOU good at?

I'm	very quite not so	good at	English art swimming football ... maths

pair work

c) Now ask three classmates and report back to your class.

B5 An interview with Claire

CD

Claire is giving an interview to a reporter from Radio Junior Europe (RJE). There is only a little time left before the semi-finals.

LiF→ 11, 12

RJE: And where will you be this time next week, Claire?

Claire: Well, I'll be in Birmingham for the semi-finals of "Ready, steady, go!"

RJE: Will the Roaring Tigers be the new champions?

Claire: I hope so. When Max plays, we can't lose.

RJE: Won't he be too slow?

Claire: Oh, Max is great. Together we'll win the championship.

RJE: Yes, but sometimes when he speaks – well, he's a little slow and this is a game for quick talkers like you.

Claire: Oh, in the game he's fine. We're not worried at all. I'll just take his hand and squeeze!

RJE: Thank you, Claire – and good luck!

Workbook

B2 – B4 ◀

B6 Is it "will" or "won't"?

1 Max ... be in Birmingham with Claire.
2 Max and Claire ... be in the semi-finals.
3 Claire thinks they ... lose.
4 Max ... be too slow.
5 Together they ... win the championship.
6 Claire ... take Max's hand and squeeze.

C1

a) Can you make a mindmap about music?

b) Look at the pictures in C2. Make a list of words that go with them. Which of your words can you find in the story?

C2   Buskers

Karim and his friend Eddy like music. They like blues, rock'n'roll and pop music. Karim plays the guitar and Eddy plays comb and paper. Eddy likes crazy hats. He already has a few really big hats and many caps in different colours.

One day Karim and Eddy want to go to the cinema.

Karim: No pocket money left! Do you have any money, Eddy?

Eddy: Only a little. Let's go and play music in Piccadilly Circus. In half an hour we'll have enough money for the cinema.

Eddy/Karim: Well, it's –
One for the money
Two for the show
Three to get ready
And go cat go!

Policeman: Now boys, how old are you? Sorry, you can't play music here, you know. Take your guitar and off you go.

Eddy: How much did we collect, Karim?
Karim: Over £10.
Eddy: Fantastic. Now we can see the film and buy an ice-cream.

C3   Now act this scene in class.

CD

LiF → 13, 14

Workbook
C1 – C5

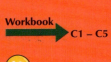

teamwork

3

Workbook
C6, C7

C4 **What about YOUR pocket money?**
Is there enough for cinema and ice-cream and CDs and …?
What can you do to earn some extra money?

Example: I can sell my old cap.

take a dog for a walk

sell my …

work in the garden for …

help …

do a paper round

babysit for …

wash the car for …

go shopping for …

water flowers for …

repair …

C5 Musical instruments

Here are some instruments that you can make at home or in the classroom.

Clapping spoons
You will need: 2 large spoons. Sit down and hold the spoons back-to-back in one hand. Put your index finger between the spoons and hold the spoons tightly. Hold your other hand over the spoons. Now hit first your leg, then your hand with the spoons.
Do it fast or slowly, make your own rhythm.

Rap shaker
You will need: an empty can, some rice, an elastic band and some paper. Clean the can. Fill it about half full with rice. Cover the opening with the paper and put an elastic band around it. Now shake the can – and you have a rap shaker.

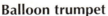

Balloon trumpet
You will need: a balloon. Blow up the balloon. Hold it closed with the thumbs and index fingers of both hands.
Pull your fingers apart and stretch the balloon opening. This will sound like a trumpet. Let the air out faster – the sound will change.

Comb and paper
You will need: a comb and some paper. Fold the paper over the teeth of the comb. Now blow onto the paper and you will make a sound.

C6 Be a busker

Here is a rock'n'roll song. Can you find a good rhythm for it?
Use your musical instruments. You can also clap your hands.
Get in groups and sing your song to the rest of the class.

teamwork

I'm going to the party
To hear the music play,
I want to dance with her
Till the break of day.

She says she will be there.
She says she loves me, too.
I want to dance with her
Till the sun comes through.

Chorus:
It's one o'clock, two o'clock,
Three o'clock, four,
It's getting very late
But I want to dance some more.
It's five o'clock, six o'clock,
Seven o'clock, eight,
The sun is coming up,
Oh, it's very, very late!

Workbook
C8

58

Shopping in the high street

4

LiF→ 3

A1 Do you remember …?

People celebrate New Year's Eve all over the world. But the customs are different. Do you remember what YOU did last New Year's Eve?

Did you …?   Yes, I/we did. / No, I/we didn't.

read a book

watch TV

drink punch

go to bed early

have a good meal

sing   let off fireworks

play games

decorate the house

wish the neighbours a happy New Year

make three wishes

go to church

go for a midnight walk

have a party

dance

I/we went for a midnight walk but I/we didn't go to church.

I/we …
and I/we …

tip

For your answers you'll need the simple past forms. You can find them on page 157.

Workbook
A1

A2   Friends from other countries

Are there pupils from other countries in YOUR class or YOUR school?
Find out what they do on New Year's Eve. Here are some questions you can ask:

– When is your New Year's Eve? What is it called?
– Do you eat special food on New Year's Eve? What do you eat?
– Do you give presents?
– Do you decorate your house? How do you decorate it?
– Do you put on special clothes?
– Do you send cards? What do you write on the cards?
– Do you dance and play music?
– What time do you go to bed?

Work in groups, find out about the festivals and report back to your class.
You can collect pictures and decorations and make a collage.
These pictures can help you plan your work.

When you work on a
project, you:
1 plan it,
2 do it,
3 check it,
4 present it.

1 In your group: Write down
       – **the questions you want to ask.**
       – **who you can ask.**
       – **when you want to start.**
       – **what you need for the interviews.**

2 On the job:
   – **Ask your questions.**
   – **Take notes and/or use a**
     cassette recorder.

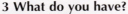

3 What do you have?
   – **Collect pictures and photos for a collage.**
   – **Use the interviews for a text/texts**
     about the festival.
   – **Your teacher will help you**
     with your English.

4 Your collage:

   – **Put texts and pictures together.**
   – **Show your collage to your class,**
     your teachers, your parents, …

NOTTING

Pu

No 125   Tuesday, 12 October

New Year for London's Asians

Most of London's Asians celebrate the New Year twice: one celebration is on 31 December. But they usually celebrate their own New Year, too. Hindus celebrate Diwali, the Festival of Lights. The god Rama comes back at that time and everyone welcomes him with lights. The girls also dance for the goddess Lakshmi – she brings good luck for the New Year. People buy little presents and make delicious things to eat like chapati – a warm bread. (See recipe on this page.) Muslims celebrate a different New Year – the Hegira. That was the time when the prophet Muhammad left the city of Mecca.

project

Chapati

You need:
750 g wholemeal flour
1 teaspoon salt
1 tablespoon vegetable oil
250 ml warm water

Put 600 g of the flour in a bowl. Add the salt and oil and mix well. Add the water and knead for about ten minutes. Leave the dough for an hour. Take out pieces of dough and form about 20 small balls. Roll them out on the rest of the flour. They are now flat. Heat oil in deep pan. When the oil is very hot, bake the chapatis one after the other until they are golden brown. You can also eat them with meat or vegetables.

ILL NEWS

70 p Weekly

in London

Karim's super candles

Schoolboy Karim Khan from Notting Hill has big plans for the festival of Diwali. Diwali starts in late October or early November. It is the beginning of the Hindu New Year. Hindus call it the Festival of Lights. They put candles and lamps in their windows to welcome the god Rama.

Computer freak Karim wants to hang up strings of coloured lights in the window of his room and join them to his stereo and computer. He is going to play Indian music and rock'n'roll – a real sound and light show! His parents just put a few candles in their windows.

Diwali Week programme

Monday:	Festival of Lights
Tuesday:	Dance at Ealing Town Hall
Wednesday:	Family dinner and party at the sports centre

A4

a) Collect words about Diwali on pages 62 and 63.
Write them down.

b) Now organize your words. Can you use them to answer these questions?

Workbook
A2, A3

WHAT is Diwali?

WHEN is Diwali?

HOW do people celebrate?

Land und Leute   Neujahrsfeste in Großbritannien

In den meisten Gegenden Großbritanniens wird am 31. Dezember Silvester so gefeiert, wie ihr es auch aus Deutschland kennt. Anders ist jedoch, dass die Briten so gut wie kein Feuerwerk zünden.

Workbook
A4, A5

Die Schotten feiern noch heute vielerorts ihr traditionelles Neujahrsfest *Hogmanay*. Wenn um Mitternacht Gewehrschüsse oder Schiffssirenen das neue Jahr ankündigen, werden die Nachbarn besucht und beschenkt: mit einer Flasche Whisky, einem Stück Kohle (zum Wärmen) und etwas Essbarem, z.B. Haferkeksen.

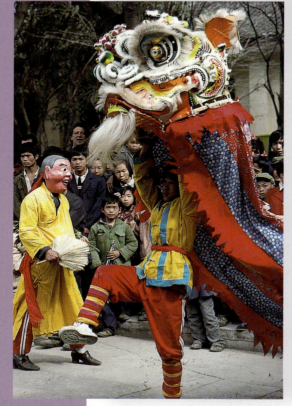

In London leben Menschen aus aller Welt. Sie haben ihre Bräuche und Feste mitgebracht. So kann man im Londoner Stadtteil Soho zwischen Mitte Januar und Mitte Februar das chinesische Neujahrsfest beobachten. Die Straßen sind dann bunt geschmückt und ein großer Umzug wird veranstaltet. An seiner Spitze befindet sich das Modell eines tanzenden Löwen, der die bösen Geister vertreiben soll. Rote Umschläge, die mit „Glücksgeld" gefüllt sind, werden an Kinder verteilt und außen an den Häusern aufgehängt. Sie sollen den Löwen anlocken und Unglück fernhalten.

A5 Presents

Sheree is going to give
her brother Karim this present:
a large glass bottle
full of coloured stones.

a) There are other things that people can give as presents.
Use the letters on the stones to write down the presents.
You can use the letters more than once.

b) Who is going to get what? Can you find out?

Chacko	
Firaki	
Cauvery	
Pradeep	is going to get the …
Chitra	
Bina	
Sheree	
Pillai	

LiF → 15, 16, 17

Workbook → A6

Workbook
B1

Workbook
B2

CD

Workbook
B3

B 1

It's Gillian's mum's birthday tomorrow.
Gillian is going to buy a present for her.

What do you think – is she going to buy
– flowers?
– a box of chocolates?
– perfume?
– a scarf?
– handkerchiefs?
– a book about tigers?
– writing paper?
– a goldfish?
– warm woolly socks?

**Collect all the guesses in
your class before you read B2.**

B 2 **A brilliant idea**

Gillian is out shopping –
it's her mum's birthday tomorrow
and Gillian wants to buy a present.
She goes to Oxford Street,
walks up and down and looks
in all the shop windows.

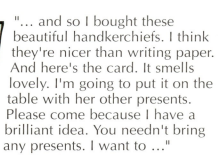

"Mmm, lovely scarf. Ah, there's a better one. Oh, no. Too expensive.
But that red one is cheaper. No, not a scarf. What shall I buy for Mum's
birthday?"

She stops outside Selfridge's, one of the largest
department stores in London. You can buy
everything there. Beautiful things – perfumes,
gloves, sunglasses, handbags. But, oh dear,
very expensive. In the stationery
department she finds a pretty birthday card –
pink and blue. No, here's a prettier one.
£2.50 and it smells of roses. Then she has
another idea. Perhaps she can buy her mum
some writing paper – but no, just a minute!

"… and so I bought these
beautiful handkerchiefs. I think
they're nicer than writing paper.
And here's the card. It smells
lovely. I'm going to put it on the
table with her other presents.
Please come because I have a
brilliant idea. You needn't bring
any presents. I want to …"

B3

a) Read B2 again and make two lists:

presents
scarf
...

what the presents are like
lovely
...

b) Find the words with these endings in your second list and write them down:

...per   ...ier   ...ter   ...cer

c) Now compare the presents in your first list like this:

LiF → 18

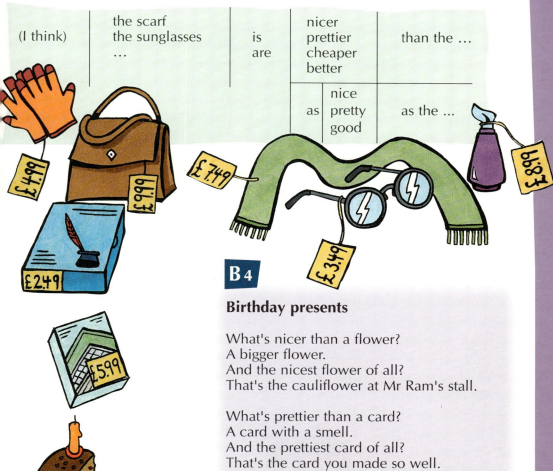

(I think)	the scarf the sunglasses ...	is are	nicer prettier cheaper better	than the ...
		as	nice pretty good	as the ...

£4.99

£7.49

£9.99

£8.99

£3.49

£2.49

£5.99

B4

Birthday presents

What's nicer than a flower?
A bigger flower.
And the nicest flower of all?
That's the cauliflower at Mr Ram's stall.

What's prettier than a card?
A card with a smell.
And the prettiest card of all?
That's the card you made so well.

What's lovelier than a cake?
A larger cake.
And the loveliest cake of all?
That's the chocolate cake you baked for me.
I'm sorry but there's only a little left.

Workbook → B4 – B6

B 5 An unusual birthday

Vera and Charlie came round to wish Mrs Collins a happy birthday. And to help Gillian with her brilliant idea.

Vera was a maid and Charlie dressed up as a butler. Gillian made a delicious meal – Indian chicken – and the maid and the butler laid the table. Mrs Collins waited.

Then the butler put a paper crown on her head and asked her to come to the table.

Mrs Collins found all her presents. She loved the handkerchiefs but thought the card smelled of oranges.

The butler served the chicken. Mrs Collins said it was the most wonderful meal. Everyone was so polite! Afterwards Mrs Collins said, "What a pity I only have one birthday a year!"

B 6

"Thanks Mum.
Yes, I had a lovely birthday.
Gillian cooked …
and Vera and Charlie helped her.
Charlie … and Vera …
Then Charlie, the butler, put …
I got …
I loved …
Charlie served …
Everyone was …"

What does Mrs Collins tell her mum? Can you go on?

C1 A strange old lady

Yesterday, an old lady came into the Superstore. She was wearing a long red raincoat and a green scarf. She had a big green hat. The scarf was greener than her hat. She had black socks and a pair of very funny shoes on her feet.

She picked up a newspaper and started to read it. Then she looked at shampoos. "Hmm. Bad for you. Too many chemicals."

She walked around the shop, picked up the cheese, squeezed the tomatoes. "Not fresh," she said. David's father watched her.

The old lady went out of the shop. But she forgot her handbag. David saw it and ran after her but he was too late.

David's father walked up to her. "Can I help you?" he asked. "Er, yes. I'm going to fly to Africa next week. Rainy season there, you know. Do you sell umbrellas?" "I'm sorry, madam," said David's father. "No umbrellas."

David and his father opened the bag and found £100 inside but no name, no address. "Wow. May we keep it, Dad?" asked David. "No, David. We must give it to the police. And I'm going to put a notice in the window." "And then?" "Well, the police will keep the bag and money for six months." "And after six months?" "I think you can keep it. But I'm sure she'll be back tomorrow."

C2 What do you think: "TRUE", "FALSE" or "DON'T KNOW"?

1 Yesterday, an old lady came into the Superstore.
2 She wanted to buy a newspaper.
3 She walked around the shop and bought some shampoo.
4 She thought the Superstore had umbrellas.
5 She forgot her basket.
6 David ran after her but couldn't find her.
7 There were papers in the handbag.
8 David wanted to keep the £100.
9 His father wanted to give the handbag to the police.
10 The old lady will be back tomorrow.

Workbook
C1, C2 ◀———

LiF → 15

C3 What are David, his dad, the old lady and the policeman going to do?

David – write – notice

1 Mr Williams – phone – police

Mr Williams – put – notice – in the shop window

Lady – go – to the police

5 Policeman – phone – Mr Williams

Lady – give David – present

LiF → 18

C4 These adjectives come from C1.
Use them to compare the nouns.

Example: The lady's scarf is greener than her hat.

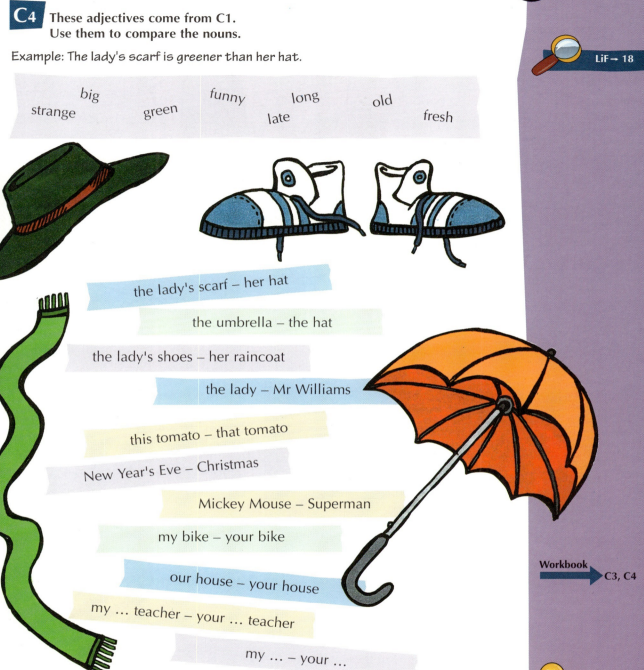

big

strange   green

funny   long   old

late   fresh

the lady's scarf – her hat

the umbrella – the hat

the lady's shoes – her raincoat

the lady – Mr Williams

this tomato – that tomato

New Year's Eve – Christmas

Mickey Mouse – Superman

my bike – your bike

our house – your house

my ... teacher – your ... teacher

my ... – your ...

Workbook ➤ C3, C4

teamwork

C5 Going shopping

Sit in a circle. One player starts and says, "I went shopping yesterday and I bought a CD." The next player says, "I went shopping yesterday and I bought a CD and a T-shirt."
A player always repeats the names of everything the players before him/her bought and adds something new.
Players who forget something or make a mistake are out of the game.

C6 Lord Stopwhistle goes shopping

Lord Stopwhistle
lives in Belgravia,
a very expensive
part of London.

One morning
he says to
his butler:

> James, I really
> must buy a present
> for Lady Stopwhistle.
> Do you have
> any idea?

> Yes, M'lord.
> You could go on
> a little shopping
> trip in a typical
> high street, sir.

> M'lord. In a typical
> high street you will find
> W.H.Smith's, sir, for books
> and stationery. Then
> there's Boots for
> cosmetics. Marks &
> Spencer, sir, always have
> lovely pullovers. And then,
> sir, there's Woolworth's.
> They have everything.

Lord Stopwhistle is very surprised. He doesn't know a British high street.
He buys his shirts at a shirtmaker's, his shoes at a shoemaker's.

So Lord Stopwhistle goes to a
typical British high street. He buys
writing paper at W.H.Smith's and a
lipstick at Boots for Lady Stopwhistle.
Then he buys a pullover at Marks &
Spencer's and a Rolling Bones' CD
at Woolworth's.

And at home:

> I say, James.
> Look at all these
> things. Fantastic.
> And do you know?
> They were very
> cheap!

Workbook
C5, C6 ←

C7 Choose one of these tasks:

– **Act the scene.**
  You can use the text from C6.
– **Write and act this shopping dialogue:**
  Lord Stopwhistle buys a
  present for Lady Stopwhistle.
– **Write and act this dialogue:**
  Lord Stopwhistle comes home.
  Lady Stopwhistle gets her presents.

Record your dialogue on a cassette.

Dos and don'ts

A1 Problems

What do you think is the problem between this boy and his mother?

The boy's …

Can you think of more problems between parents and children?

Workbook
A1

CD

LiF → 20

A2 Mum's rules

Last summer Gillian met Lisa Naumann in London.
Now they are penfriends.
They often write letters.
Sometimes they write about nice things but sometimes they write about their problems …

What can you find out about Gillian? What can you find out about her mother?

these red earrings were more expensive but I love the colour. I can't wear them at school but I'll wear them at Roger's party next week. He's the most interesting boy in my class. Perhaps I'll wear my new lip gloss, too. It's pink. Mum mustn't see it. She has all those silly rules: what I have to do, what I mustn't do, what I can wear, what I can't wear. What are your parents like? Do they make silly rules, too? Can you stay up late? Can you go to discos? Can you wear what you like when

Workbook
A2, A3

A3 Gillian writes about her problems with her mum.
What about YOU?

Use your list of problems from A1 again and talk about them:
Here are some examples. You can also make your own sentences.

I have to …   I mustn't …   I can …   I can't …

… wear	earrings my old jeans what I want	when I go	to school. out in the afternoon. to visit my grandmother.

… dye my hair.
… do my homework before I can …
… watch TV after … o'clock.
… go to the cinema.
… play on my computer before I do
   my homework.

… listen to my CDs in the
   living-room.
… buy cosmetics.
… eat sweets before dinner.
…

 A4

a) What did Gillian write about at the beginning of her letter?
Listen to the CD and find out how she bought the earrings.

Gillian and Vera look
at red, blue and bird earrings.
First they talk about the … earrings.
Then they talk about the … earrings.
At the end they talk about the … earrings.
How much are Gillian's earrings?

b) Compare the earrings:

The … earrings are	more	colourful beautiful expensive	than the …

c) Do you like earrings?
What do your favourite earrings look like?
Describe them to a partner.

 LiF→ 21

Workbook A4, A5

 CD

 LiF→ 19

Workbook A6

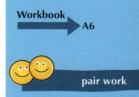 pair work

LiF→ 19

portfolio

A5 My personal tastes

Write a list of YOUR personal tastes. The pictures can give you some ideas:

School subjects
boring:
more boring:
most boring:

English tests are difficult.
... tests are more difficult.
... tests are most difficult.

Toys
expensive:
more expensive:
most expensive:

Tests at school
difficult:
more difficult:
most difficult:

Books
interesting:
more interesting:
most interesting:

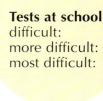

Favourite films
exciting:
more exciting:
most exciting:

Favourite food
delicious:
more delicious:
most delicious:

Workbook
A7 ←

A6 Records, records

There are many world records. Here are some examples from the Guinness Book of Records.

Make sentences like this:

dog – old – 29 years, 9 months:
The oldest dog was 29 years and 9 months.

animal – dangerous – malaria mosquito:
The most dangerous animal is the malaria mosquito.

1   car – expensive – £400,000
2   snowman – high – 29.43 m
3   chewing gum bubble – large – 58.4 cm
4   singer – successful – Madonna
5   animal – large – blue whale
6   hamburger – heavy – 2,270.66 kg
7   man – tall – 2.72 m
8   cake – large – 58.08 tons
9   ballpoint – expensive – over £22,000
10 snake – long – 10 m

Can you find more records?
Think of rivers, mountains,
cities, countries …

tip

You can find more information on the internet, for example http://www.altonweb.com/history/wadlow

LiF → 18, 19

Workbook
→ A8

pair work

teamwork

LiF→ 21

B1 Rules – rules – rules

You have rules at home and you have rules at school.

**a) Think of rules at YOUR school and in YOUR class.
Write them down with a partner:**

I/we must …   I/we mustn't …

**b) Work with another pair. Compare your rules first.
Then put them in two groups:**

<u>OK</u>   <u>not OK</u>
I/we must …   I/we must …
I/we mustn't …   I/we mustn't …

B2 At school

Don't Mess about in a Science lab!!!
By Louta Rawks!

HENDON SCHOOL RULES

1 Pupils must be polite and respect the school rules.
2 Pupils must be in school by 8.45am. Pupils who are late must go to the deputy head first.
3 Pupils must not run in the school building.
4 All pupils in years 7 to 11 must wear school uniform. White shirt, dark blue pullover and blazer, school tie and grey trousers for boys and dark blue skirt or trousers for girls. Pupils must not wear jeans or miniskirts at school.
5 Pupils must wear sports gear for sports.
6 Pupils must not smoke.
7 Pupils must not wear any make-up.
8 Pupils must not bring any pets to school.
9 Pupils must stay in the school grounds at break and at lunch time.
10 Pupils can eat school dinner or bring packed lunches. Pupils who eat special diets must bring a note to the deputy head.

Find all the words
for clothes in the
school rules.

B 3 No problem?

Read the school rules to answer these questions:

1 David's alarm clock didn't work. He gets to school at 9am.
  What must he do?
2 Nasaar wants to wear her new miniskirt to school. She is in year 8.
  Can she or can't she?
3 Charlie wants to play hockey after school. What must he bring with him?
4 Pat is wearing her new lipgloss. Is that a problem?
5 David doesn't like the school dinner on Tuesday. What can he bring?
6 Robin is a vegetarian but he wants to eat a school dinner.
  What must he do?
7 Sue wants to interview some people for the school newspaper at
  lunchtime. Can she leave the school grounds?

Workbook → **B3, B4**

Land und Leute Schuluniformen

Viele Schülerinnen und Schüler in Großbritannien tragen
eine Schuluniform. Für Mädchen ist das oft ein dunkler
Rock und eine Bluse mit Schulkrawatte oder im Sommer
ein helles Kleid. Jungen tragen eine dunkle Hose und ein
Hemd mit Krawatte.

An den meisten Schulen kommen Pullover oder Sweatshirts und Blazer mit dem Abzeichen der Schule dazu. So
kann auf der Straße jeder auf den ersten Blick erkennen,
von welcher Schule jemand kommt.

Nur wenige Jungen und Mädchen sind gegen diese Uniform. Sie gehört eben zum Schulleben. Außerdem gibt es
so auch keinen Streit über die Jeans- oder Turnschuhmarke,
das teuerste Sweatshirt usw.

Großbritannien ist übrigens nicht das einzige Land mit Schuluniformen. Es gibt sie
z.B. auch in Italien, Argentinien und in
der Türkei. Sicher findet ihr noch
mehr Länder, wenn ihr eure
ausländischen
Mitschüler
fragt.

B 4 Look at these pupils from Holland Park School.
What must they wear at school? The text in B2 can help you.

B 5 What do YOU and YOUR friends wear when you go to school?

| I/we | usually
often
sometimes
never | wear …
put on … |
|---|---|---|

What do YOU think about school uniforms?

| I think it's | better
worse
cheaper
more expensive
nicer
more boring
… | to wear | jeans
uniforms
sweatshirts
miniskirts
… | at school. |
|---|---|---|---|---|

Workbook
B5 – B7 ◄

Now have a vote in your class:
Hands up: Who's for/against school uniforms?

C1 Look at the picture in C2. Read the headline and try to understand what it is about. Do not use your dictionary.

Is the picture about
– school uniforms?
– school rules?
– safe cycling?
– a game for children?

C2 **Keep on the safe side**

a) **What rules are the people breaking here? How many can you find?**

b) **Tell the people in the picture what they must or mustn't do.**

> Person A:
> You mustn't
> carry a
> passenger.

You	must mustn't	carry a passenger.
		carry a child in a special seat.
		hold on to another person.
		keep your hands on the handlebar.
		keep both wheels of your bike on the ground.
		have your saddle too high or too low.
		wear a helmet.
		have reflectors on your wheels.

tip

Look at the bike on page 86 for help.

Workbook
C1

Land und Leute   **Linksverkehr**

Wichtig nicht nur für Autofahrer: In Großbritannien herrscht Linksverkehr. Die Briten und die Iren sind die Einzigen in Europa, die links fahren. Außerhalb von Europa wird in vielen Ländern links gefahren, z.B. in Indien, Australien, Singapur, Jamaica, in einigen afrikanischen Ländern und in dem Land, das heute die meisten Autos herstellt: Japan. In diesen Ländern ist das Lenkrad rechts im Auto. Kinder in Deutschland lernen schon im Kindergarten: "Schau links, dann rechts, dann geradeaus, dann kommst du sicher gut nach Haus." Was lernen britische Kinder wohl? Besucher in London werden gewarnt, weil viele automatisch in die falsche Richtung sehen. Für sie tragen viele Straßen deutlich in weißer Farbe die Aufschrift: *Look right.*

C3

Up the hill – higher and higher
I pedal hard – slower and slower
Then down again – faster and faster
Look! I can fly – lower and lower

Watch out! A tree!

C4 In the street

There is a policewoman at Hendon School. She goes there every month to give road safety lessons to years 7 and 8. Today she is telling pupils about traffic signs:

"It's very important to look at the traffic signs when you are in the street. Some signs are for people on foot or for people on bikes. The signs for motorists are important for you, too.
Look at the signs when you cross the road.
Now – you are out on your bike and see sign number one.
You mustn't ride your bike here – so get off!
Sign number two means you can't ride into that street. Now, sign number three means that a cyclist or motorist must turn left. And what about sign number four? –
Yes, you must turn right.
And here's sign number five –
you mustn't turn right here.
And when you see this sign, number six, you must stop and be very careful."

C5 Traffic signs

Look at the six traffic signs and say what you must or mustn't do.

Stop!

Turn left!

Turn right!

Don't turn right!

Don't ride into this street!

Don't ride your bike here!

I know this is sign
. . . .
I must/mustn't
. . .

Can you draw four other signs and say what they mean?

Workbook
C2, C3

C6 A safe bike

What is a safe bike?
Look at the picture and use the words.

A safe bike must have …

good   well-oiled
        clean
strong   working

saddle   handlebar   bell

pump

light   light

reflector   reflector

brake   brake

                          tyre

gears   wheel

tyre   reflector
wheel

chain

pedal

Workbook
C4, C5

portfolio

C7 My bike

I love my bike. It has 21 gears. I can ride my bike to school and in the evenings I can cycle to the sports club. At weekends my friends and I clean and repair our bikes. When everything is clean and well-oiled and working we ride up and down the streets or we have races in the park.
People sometimes shout at us then. What about a track just for bikers?

What can YOU write about YOUR bike?

School's out!

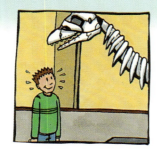

A1

a) **Look at the picture in the story on this page. Guess:**
– Which country do you think it is?
– Who is in the story?
– Is the picture the beginning / the middle / the end of the story?

b) **Draw two or three more pictures for the story before you read.**
What do you think happens?

Workbook
A1

CD

A2 **Rocky Mountain adventure**

… and here is Jack Wilkins, your RMX reporter. I'm flying with Ranger
Schablonsky from the National Park Service. We're out here in the
Rockies and we're looking for a balloon pilot.

Visitors saw a balloon yesterday. It was landing in the trees and so they
called the rangers. We're sure the man is alive but he's out here in
real grizzly country. And – wait a minute! There he is! Gee, he's
in a tree! And there's a grizzly running away! With her cubs!
Wow! Listeners, this is RMX, Jack Wilkins reporting. We've
found the man. Yes, we're sending down a rope with a
microphone at the end of it. And he's caught it! An
exclusive interview with RMX and a balloon pilot in a tree
in the Rockies! Hi! Can you hear me?

Mr Graham: Yes, I can. Are you going to pull me out of here?

Jack Wilkins: In a minute, in a minute. Now your name is …?

Mr Graham: John Graham. I'm from London. Can you get me out
of here?

Jack Wilkins: Yes, yes. Is that London, England? That's great. Just great.
Have you ever visited the Rockies before?

Mr Graham: No, never. I want to get out of here!

Jack Wilkins: Can you tell the RMX listeners why you are in a tree in the
middle of the Rockies?

Mr Graham: Well, I fell into it. In my balloon. And I want out! Now!

Jack Wilkins: How long have you been there?

Mr Graham: I've been here for eighteen hours. I was flying too low
and the trees are very high here. I'm OK but I'm very hungry. I'd love
to have a cup of tea because I've had nothing to eat or drink for hours.
I've lost everything. And I've caught a terrible cold! And I want out!

Jack Wilkins: Yeah, yeah. We'll get you out of there soon.
Don't worry. Tell us about the bears.

Mr Graham: Well, a bear was at the bottom of the tree all the
time. Sometimes with cubs. She tried to climb the tree – that's
why I couldn't climb down.

Jack Wilkins: Don't worry. Grizzlies can't climb. Now here's
Ranger Schablonsky. He's going to pull you out.

Ranger Schablonsky: OK now. You see that red rope?
Well …

Workbook
A2

A3

a) Read the text again and find
- the name of an animal and of its babies.
- different words for people.
- different words to do with interviews.
- information about Mr Graham.

b) Write down these sentences in the right order.
They will tell you Mr Graham's adventure in short.

Workbook A3

He couldn't climb down because a grizzly bear wanted to climb up.
Mr Graham flew his balloon over the Rocky Mountains.
A park ranger pulled him out of the tree.
After 18 hours a helicopter found him.
Mr Graham was flying too low.
There were very high trees.
Then he fell into a tree.

Land und Leute Die Rocky Mountains

Was wisst ihr über die USA? Sicher eine ganze Menge. Sammelt doch einmal in eurer Klasse, was euch dazu einfällt. Sind die Rocky Mountains auch in eurer Sammlung enthalten? Sie gehören unbedingt dazu: 487 Gesangsvereine, 224 Hotels, 188 Schiffe und 26 Züge sind nach ihnen benannt. Könnt ihr herausfinden, was Rocky Mountains auf Deutsch heißt?

Die Rockies ziehen sich durch den Westen der USA, vom Yukon in Alaska bis zum Rio Grande del Norte in Mexiko.

Rocky Mountain National Park, Colorado

Sie sind mit 5.500 km das zweitlängste Gebirge der Erde.
Der höchste Berg ist der Mount McKinley mit 6.200 m, außerdem gibt es noch einige Viertausender. Sucht sie doch einmal im Atlas, schreibt ihre genaue Höhe auf und in welchem Bundesstaat der USA sie liegen.

Viele Gebiete der Rockies sind so schön, dass sie zu Naturschutzgebieten gemacht wurden. Am bekanntesten ist der Yellowstone Nationalpark mit seinen heißen Springquellen (Geysiren). Im Sequoia Nationalpark in Kalifornien gibt es riesige, mehr als 3.500 Jahre alte Mammutbäume. Der Yosemite Nationalpark ist für seine Wasserfälle berühmt.

A coyote

In den Rockies kann man vielen Tieren begegnen: z.B. Präriewölfen *(coyotes)*, Dickhornschafen *(bighorns)* und ab und zu einem Grizzlybären *(grizzly bear)*.

A4 Did you know?

Grizzly bears can be about 2.20 m tall. They are very strong. Don't talk to a grizzly when it's going for a walk with its family. Grizzlies always attack when they think their family is in danger.

Workbook
A4 ⬅

Grizzly bears don't like noise. In the Rockies, the men looking for gold always make a lot of noise to keep the bears away.

Grizzly bears don't like climbing trees. So climb a tree when YOU meet one. The grizzly will try to pull it out of the ground.

Grizzly with cubs

Yellowstone National Park, Wyoming

pair work

LiF→ 22 – 24

A5 Work with a partner, ask questions and answer them. Find out six things you have done but your partner hasn't done.

> Have you ever been to …?
> Have you ever visited …?

> Yes, I have. /
> No, I haven't.

**Find more questions.
You can also use these words:**

had   watched

   played   found

caught   met

   cleaned   listened to

> Have you ever met a grizzly?

> Have you ever played hockey?

> Have you ever had snails for lunch?

> Have you ever watched a science fiction programme?

Workbook
A5 ⬅

Can you also think of funny questions?

> Have you ever talked to a hippo?

> Have you ever met a teacher in boxer shorts?

B1 Dinosaurs

a) Do you know what dinosaurs look like? They lived millions of years ago. Take some paper and draw YOUR idea of a dinosaur. Hang up the pictures in your classroom.

b) Can you write down what YOUR dinosaur looks like, what it is like and what it can do? You can use these words:

adjectives	nouns	verbs
small	animal	eat
big	body	walk
long	tail	fight
strong	feet	drink
dangerous	neck	sleep
brown	head	have
green	teeth	be
friendly	legs	swim
unfriendly	ears	kill
funny	plants	fly
...	meat	roar
...	...	...
...	...	...

tip

Find information about dinosaurs at home, in a library, or on the internet.

Workbook B1

CD

B2 A very special dinosaur

Charlie would love to buy a present for Lisa Naumann because he likes her very much. He wants to take it with him when he visits her in the summer holidays.

And he has an idea. Lisa sent him a model dinosaur last year – Terry the tyrannosaurus. She collects dinosaurs and now Charlie is interested in them, too. He often goes to the Natural History Museum. There is a good shop where you can buy models and books.

Charlie wants to find something special, extra special, extra dinosaury for Lisa. But what can he buy? There are dinosaur models and posters and books and puzzles and pens and many other things. Everything about dinosaurs. Perhaps a book in English is too difficult. She is interested in horses. She likes going to other countries. She likes music. She likes ice-skating. She can play the piano. She is good at making things.

Do you have a dinosaur that skates on ice and can play the piano? Oh, and looks like a horse?

Workbook B2

B 3 You can learn a lot about Lisa and about Charlie in B2.
Choose Lisa or Charlie and collect information about them.

Lisa: She sent Charlie a model dinosaur. She collects dinosaurs. ...

Charlie: Charlie would love to buy ... . He likes ... .

Workbook
B3 ←

pair work

B 4 What are YOU interested in?
Work with a partner. Ask him/her if he/she is interested in these things:

Are you
interested in ...?

hamsters	music
horses	computers
goldfish	stamps
English	table tennis
history	make-up
wild animals	dinosaurs
books	films
football	...

Yes, I love it/them.
Yes, quite a lot .
Not much.
No, I'm not. I hate it/them.

I think it's /
they're ...

What about you?
Are you interested in ...?

Make a survey in
your class.
Find out what people
are interested in.

Workbook
B4, B5 ←

pair work

B 5 Things you'd love to do

Charlie says, "I'd love to buy a fantastic present for Lisa because I like her."
What would YOU love to do?

I'd love to ...	because ...
ride a horse	I can buy everything I want.
eat ...	I like ...
fly in a helicopter	I'm ...
go up in a balloon	I've never tried it/them.
have a lot of money	I want to be famous.
be in a TV show	I want to see ...
have ...	it's exciting.
go ...	it's a beautiful animal.
meet ...	you can see a lot.
...	...

Work with a partner. Tell him/her what YOU would love to do and why.

B6 The baby supersaurus

It was a very hot Saturday afternoon. Charlie was in the Natural History Museum. He was looking at the skeleton of a supersaurus. It was a very big skeleton.

Suddenly, there was a noise. Not a loud noise. Crack – cr-a-ck – cr-a-a-ck. Charlie walked around the skeleton. What was making the noise? There was nothing to see.

A man walked into the room and he heard the noise, too. He ran to the skeleton and asked Charlie, "Can you see it? Can you see it?"
"See what?" asked Charlie.
"The egg. There must be an egg," said the man. Now he was looking under the skeleton. Charlie was still walking around the skeleton. He saw nothing but the noise was getting louder.

"What are we looking for?" Charlie asked the man. The man looked at him. "There is an egg here. A dinosaur egg. And … oh, dear me! My name is Professor Goodbody. I put the egg there about three weeks ago. But now I can't find it. Help me, please."

Charlie looked again, this time between the big feet of the skeleton. Something was moving there. It was green, a green head. Then there was a long green neck. A loud crack – and the rest of the baby dinosaur came out of the egg. It was a baby supersaurus.

"I've found it! It's here!" shouted Charlie. "Help! It's running out of the room!"
"Hey, no running in here!" A museum guide stopped Charlie.

Workbook ➤ B6

"There's a baby dinosaur and it's running out onto the street," said Charlie.
"Now, now, I think you've had too much sun. Cool down," said the guide.
"But Professor Goodbody! He saw it, too!" shouted Charlie.
"Sorry, son. Look: the room's empty. Just you and good old Supy. Come on, now."

Charlie walked out into the street. It was a very hot Saturday afternoon.

6

... take the dog for a long walk

C1 Holidays at last!

What are YOU going to do in the holidays?

... lie in the sun

... go to a museum

... clean my room

... sleep in a tent in the garden

I'm going to	fly	
	go	to ...
	visit	
	sleep	
	swim	...
	take	
	ride	
	...	

C2 Summer holidays!

It's the first day of the summer holidays and Susan and Karim are sitting in Kensington Gardens – alone! All their friends are on holiday. Charlie is in Germany with Lisa and her parents. He has found a wonderful present for Lisa. David is in Wales. He has been there before. He has read a book about castles and wants to visit some of them. Gillian and her mum have invited Vera to come with them to Cornwall. Mrs Collins has bought a tent and they all hope to have good weather. It's not much fun in a tent when it rains.

Now Susan and Karim are thinking about what they can do in the holidays. Perhaps they could go swimming. Or they could go to a pop concert. Or they could visit a museum. Or ...

C3

Susan and Karim		read	a book about castles.
Charlie		bought	to Wales before.
Mrs Collins	has	been	at home.
David	have	found	Vera to Cornwall.
Gillian and her mum		invited	a present for Lisa.
		stayed	a tent.

LiF → 15

Workbook
C1, C2

LiF → 22 – 24

Workbook
C3 – C6

project

C4 YOUR cassette

Now that you have learned so much English, you can make an interesting cassette or a video. Start with your name and how old you are and then
- record the sounds and speak about interesting things in your town.
- introduce your favourite pets/animals.
- talk about your favourite book/film.
- talk about how you celebrate birthdays and special days in the year.
- play and talk about your favourite music.
- talk about your plans for the holidays.

Take your cassette recorder or your camcorder and go.
Keep your cassette for the first day of school and surprise everyone.

What do you remember?

What does Karim's friend Eddy like to wear?
What did Robin Hood do?
Where does Mr Graham have a balloon adventure?
What is Diwali?
Who gave Mrs Collins an unusual birthday present?

Who wanted to fly to Africa?
Whose mother has silly rules?
Who are the Roaring Tigers?
Who saw the Loch Ness monster?
Who won the pony camp race?

Where was the tiger?
How tall can grizzly bears be?
Who is Lisa Naumann?
What does Lord Stopwhistle buy for Lady Stopwhistle?
Who took photos in the park?

What is the name of Patsy Mulloy's pony?
At what time do the flamingos eat in the zoo?
Who is Jack Wilkins?
Who must wear a school uniform at Hendon School?
Where do you look first when you cross a road in Britain?

Where did Charlie go to find a present for Lisa?
Where did Karim and Eddy play music?
Who went shopping at Selfridge's?
What is a rap shaker?
What did Professor Goodbody
 put in the museum?

Im LiF-Anhang wird die englische Grammatik ganz genau unter die Lupe genommen.
Du kennst das längst aus Band 1: Immer, wenn du das Lupen-Symbol vorn im Buch siehst, kannst du hier im Anhang nachsehen, welche Regeln es für die englische Sprache gibt.

Hier findest du auch **Grammatik-Lerntipps** mit nützlichen Hinweisen, Tricks und Spielideen. Sie helfen dir, die Grammatikregeln besser zu verstehen und zu behalten. Probiere doch zuerst einmal verschiedene Möglichkeiten aus. Vielleicht kannst du einen Weg herausfinden, der dir persönlich am besten beim Lernen hilft.
Grammatik-Lerntipps sehen so aus:

> *tip:*
> Veranstaltet doch einmal eine Tauschbörse für Grammatik-Lerntipps in der Klasse. Dazu schreibt oder malt jede/r ihren/seinen persönlichen Lieblings-Tipp auf ein Blatt oder Poster. Dann gehen alle herum und erklären sich gegenseitig ihre Tipps. Vielleicht ist ja etwas dabei, das für dich neu und besonders hilfreich ist.

Für den Fall, dass du dich einmal an Regeln aus Band 1 nicht mehr so genau erinnerst, helfen dir die *remember*-Zettel auf die Sprünge. Hier folgt auch gleich das erste Beispiel:

remember:
simple present – Die einfache Gegenwart

- Gewohnheiten
- regelmäßig vorkommende Ereignisse

I play
you play
he play**s**
she play**s**
it play**s**
we play
you play
they play

**He, she, it –
-s must fit.**

- Besonderheiten:
  I wash – he/she/it wash**es**
  I do – he/she/it do**es**
  I go – he/she/it go**es**
  I tidy – he/she/it tid**ies**

- Verneinung mit **don't/doesn't**:
  I **don't** eat potatoes.
  He **doesn't** like cheese.

1

1 simple past (1) – Die einfache Vergangenheit

- Wenn du über Ereignisse oder Handlungen sprechen willst, die vergangen und abgeschlossen sind, benutzt du die einfache Vergangenheit *(simple past)*:

> I stayed at home in the holidays.

Im Deutschen gibt es mehrere Möglichkeiten, diese Zeit auszudrücken:

I stayed at home in the holidays. *Ich blieb in den Ferien zu Hause.*
                                    Ich bin in den Ferien zu Hause geblieben.

a) regular verbs – Regelmäßige Verben

- Die Vergangenheitsform bildest du, indem du an den Infinitiv des Verbs **-ed** anhängst:

Charlie clean**ed** the stables.   *Charlie machte die Ställe sauber.*
He look**ed** after the ponies.   *Er kümmerte sich um die Ponys.*
The girls visit**ed** a lot of friends. *Die Mädchen besuchten viele Freunde.*

- Auf **he**, **she**, **it** brauchst du dabei nicht zu achten, denn es gibt nur eine einzige Vergangenheitsform für alle Personen.

- Bei Verben, die im Infinitiv auf **-e** enden, wird nur ein **-d** angehängt:

  bake ➜ I bake**d** a cake for my mother.
           Ich habe meiner Mutter einen Kuchen gebacken.

- Bei manchen Verben ändert sich die Schreibweise, wenn **-ed** angehängt wird:

  stop ➜ The pony stop**ped** and looked at the flowers.
           Das Pony hielt an und schaute die Blumen an.

  tidy ➜ Yesterday Charlie tid**ied** his room.
           Charlie hat gestern sein Zimmer aufgeräumt.

b) irregular verbs – Unregelmäßige Verben

- Viele Verben bilden die Vergangenheitsform nicht mit **-ed**. Sie sind unregelmäßig. Ihre Formen musst du wie Vokabeln lernen. Eine Liste findest du auf Seite 157.

- **be** hat als einziges englisches Verb zwei Vergangenheitsformen: **was** und **were**.

I	**was**	*ich war*
you	**were**	*du warst, Sie waren*
he	**was**	*er war*
she	**was**	*sie war*
it	**was**	*es war*
we	**were**	*wir waren*
you	**were**	*ihr wart, Sie waren*
they	**were**	*sie waren*

- Die Vergangenheitsform von **have** ist **had** und die von **do** ist **did**.

- Weitere unregelmäßige Verben findest du in diesen Sätzen:

Charlie **went** to a pony camp.   *Charlie fuhr in ein Reitercamp.*
He **saw** a lot of ponies.   *Er sah viele Ponys.*
Two ponies **left** the racecourse.   *Zwei Ponys verließen die Rennbahn.*

- Wie findest du heraus, ob ein Verb regelmäßig oder unregelmäßig ist?
  Ganz einfach: Du schaust in der Liste der unregelmäßigen Verben nach.
  Wenn es dort nicht steht,
  ist es ein regelmäßiges Verb.

tip:
In Theme 1 lernst du, das *simple past* zu gebrauchen. Mit dem „Sehtest"-Spiel macht das Lernen der Verbformen zu Zweit Spaß. Schreibt den Infinitiv eines Verbs in großer Schrift auf ein Blatt Papier, dann die Vergangenheitsform in kleiner Schrift darunter. Stellt mehrere solcher „Sehtest"-Bögen her.
Nun stellt sich ein Partner an ein Ende des Raums und der zweite an das andere Ende. Einer hält einen Sehtest hoch und der andere muss zuerst den Infinitiv vorlesen und danach die Vergangenheit nennen. Wenn er die Vergangenheitsform nicht auswendig weiß, geht er so weit auf den Partner zu, bis er sie lesen kann.

2 simple past (2) – Sätze mit „not"

- Wenn du sagen willst, was in der Vergangenheit *nicht* geschehen ist, brauchst du **not** oder die Kurzform **-n't**, die an **was/were** angehängt wird:

Charlie was**n't** in the race.   *Charlie war nicht im Rennen.*
The ponies were**n't** hungry.   *Die Ponys waren nicht hungrig.*

- Wenn im Satz kein **was/were** vorkommt, musst du **didn't** vor das Verb stellen. Das Verb selbst lässt du dann im Infinitiv, weil **didn't** schon die Vergangenheit anzeigt.

Susan **didn't** go away for her holidays.   *Susan ist in den Ferien nicht weggefahren.*
Sunflower **didn't** cross the finishing line.   *Sunflower kam nicht ins Ziel.*

3 simple past (3) – Ja/Nein-Fragen

● Ja/Nein-Fragen mit **was/were** bildest du, indem du **was** oder **were** an den Satzanfang stellst:

Was Charlie the commentator?	**Yes**, he **was**.
Was Charlie in the race?	**No**, he **wasn't**.
Were the ponies hungry?	**No**, they **weren't**.

● In Sätzen ohne **was/were** steht **did** am Satzanfang:

Did you go camping?	**Yes**, we **did**.
Did Terry win the race?	**No**, he **didn't**.

4 simple past (4) – Fragen mit Fragewort

● Bei Fragen mit Fragewort steht zuerst das Fragewort, dann folgt **did**:

Where did you go for your holidays?	*Wo warst du in den Ferien?*
What did you do?	*Was hast du gemacht?*

● Oder **was/were**:

What was the weather like?	*Wie war das Wetter?*

5 present progressive (1) – Die Verlaufsform der Gegenwart

● Um zu sagen, was gerade passiert, nimmst du die Verlaufsform:

My dad is playing football.

● Im Deutschen gibt es diese Form nicht. Vera müsste sagen:

Mein Vater spielt gerade Fußball. oder: *Hier ist mein Vater beim Fußballspielen.*

● Die Verlaufsform bildest du so:

Form von *be (am/is/are)* + Infinitiv + *ing*

I	**am**	**writing** this letter in school.
You	**are**	**listening** to RJE.
He	**is**	**looking** for somewhere to land.
She	**is**	**enjoying** the festival.
It	**is**	**landing** in the water.
We	**are**	**collecting** empty drink cans.
You	**are**	**lying** in the sun.
They	**are**	**swimming** in the water.

remember:
personal pronouns – Personalpronomen

	possessive	*object*
I	my	me
you	your	you
he	his	him
she	her	her
it	its	it
we	our	us
you	your	you
they	their	them

● Vorsicht bei der Schreibung:

write ➜ writ**ing**   swim ➜ swim**ming**

6 present progressive (2) – Sätze mit „not"

● Wenn du Sätze in der Verlaufsform verneinen willst, musst du **not** oder die Kurzform **n't** zwischen **am**, **is, are** und das Verb in der **ing**-Form stellen:

I**'m not collecting** empty drink cans.
He **isn't lying** in the sun.
We **aren't listening** to Radio Junior Europe.

7 present progressive (3) – Ja/Nein-Fragen

- Ja/Nein-Fragen in der Verlaufsform der Gegenwart beginnen mit **am**, **is** oder **are**:

Is the dog **playing**, too?
Spielt der Hund auch?

Yes, it is. / **No, it isn't.**
Ja. / *Nein.*

Are you just **coming** out of the castle?
Kommt ihr gerade aus dem Schloss?

Yes, we are. / **No, we aren't.**
Ja. / *Nein.*

8 present progressive (4) – Fragen mit Fragewort

What is Charlie doing over there?

Was macht Charlie da drüben?

Where is the tiger walking now?
How are they trying to catch it?

Wo läuft der Tiger jetzt umher?
Wie versuchen sie ihn zu fangen?

9 Kurzantworten

- Ja/Nein-Fragen werden normalerweise mit kurzen Sätzen beantwortet:

Do hamsters eat carrots?
Fressen Hamster Möhren?

Yes, they **do**. / No, they **don't**.
Ja. / *Nein.*

Does a tiger eat meat?
Frisst ein Tiger Fleisch?

Yes, it **does**. / No, it **doesn't**.
Ja. / *Nein.*

Did you see Tower Bridge?
Hast du die Tower Bridge gesehen?

Yes, I **did**. / No, I **didn't**.
Ja. / *Nein.*

- Dabei wiederholst du **do**, **does** oder **did** aus der Frage. Einfach nur „**Yes**" oder „**No**" zu antworten, wäre etwas unhöflich.

10 Zukunft mit „will" – Das „will"-Futur

- Wenn du darüber sprechen möchtest, was in der Zukunft passieren wird, benutzt du das „will"-Futur:

I **will fly** to the moon.   Ich werde zum Mond fliegen.
David thinks he **will be** an astronaut.   David denkt, er wird Astronaut.

- Das „will"-Futur bildest du mit **will** und dem Infinitiv des Verbs. **will** ist in allen Personen gleich.

	I		
	you		
	he		
One day	she	**will**	live on the moon.
	it		
	we		
	you		
	they		

- Vorsicht! **will** sieht aus wie das deutsche Wort „will". Aber es bedeutet „werden", nicht „wollen". Im Deutschen kannst du es oft ganz weglassen, aber niemals im Englischen:

Next time I**'ll** catch you.   Das nächste Mal krieg ich dich!
                                            Das nächste Mal werde ich dich kriegen!

- Du siehst schon: Auch **will** hat eine Kurzform. Sie lautet **'ll**:

Then he**'ll** fly to Mars.   Dann fliegt er zum Mars.

Perhaps I'll be the first man on Mars.

Vielleicht werde ich der erste Mensch auf dem Mars sein.

11 „will not"

- Wenn du sagen möchtest, was *nicht* geschehen wird, benutzt du **will not** oder die Kurzform **won't**:

David **will not** be the first man on Mars.
David wird nicht der erste Mensch auf dem Mars sein.

Max **won't** be too slow in the semi-finals.

Max wird im Halbfinale nicht zu langsam sein.

12 Fragen mit „will"

Will I live on the moon one day?	**Yes**, you **will**. / **No**, you **won't**.
Werde ich eines Tages auf dem Mond leben?	*Ja.* / *Nein.*
Will they be the new champions?	**Yes**, they **will**. / **No**, they **won't**.
Werden sie die neuen Champions sein?	*Ja.* / *Nein.*

remember:

Fragen mit **will** bildest du genauso wie Fragen mit **do/does**, z.B.
   Do you play volleyball?
Weitere Beispiele findest du auf S.102, Nr. 9.

tip:
In Theme 3 lernst du das „will"-Futur kennen. Die Regel für seine Bildung kannst du in Sätzen aufschreiben. Du kannst dir aber auch verschiedene Bildchen für die einzelnen Satzelemente ausdenken und eine Regel in Bildern aufmalen.
Beispiel:

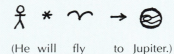

(He will fly to Jupiter.)

13 „how much" – „a little"

- Mit **how much** kannst du nach der Menge fragen:

How much money do you have, Eddy?	*Wie viel Geld hast du, Eddy?*
Only **a little**.	*Nur ein wenig.*

14 „how many" – „a few"

- Mit **how many** kannst du nach der Anzahl von Dingen fragen:

How many pounds do you have?	*Wie viele Pfund hast du?*
Just **a few**.	*Nur ein paar. / Nur einige (wenige).*

15 Zukunft mit „going to" – „going to"-Futur

● Du kannst die Zukunft mit **going to** benutzen, wenn du sagen willst, was jemand plant oder was vorauszusehen ist:

Karim **is going to play** Indian music and rock'n'roll.
Karim wird indische Musik und Rock'n'Roll spielen.

David **is going to write** a notice for the shop window.
David wird eine Notiz für das Ladenfenster schreiben.

● Die Zukunft mit **going to** bildest du so:

Form von *be (am/is/are)* + *going to* + Infinitiv

I'm		**fly** to Africa next week.
You're		**get** a lovely present.
He's		**put** a notice in the window.
She's	**going to**	**go** to the police.
It's		**rain** tomorrow.
We're		**phone** the police.
You're		**work** on a project.
They're		**go** to the family dinner.

16 „not going to"

● **not** in einen Satz mit **going to** einzubauen ist ganz leicht: **not** steht immer hinter **am**, **is** oder **are**.

I'm **not**		
She **isn't**	**going to fly** to Africa next week.
We **aren't**		

17 Fragen mit „going to"

● Wie bei allen Ja/Nein-Fragen mit **am**, **is** oder **are** rückt auch hier die Form von **be** an den Satzanfang:

Are you **going to come** to my mum's birthday party?
Kommst du zu der Geburtstagsfeier meiner Mutter?

Is Bina **going to get** the poster?
Bekommt Bina das Poster?

18 Vergleichsformen (1) – „cheap, cheaper, cheapest"

● Ein Adjektiv sagt, wie eine Sache ist:

The grey cap is **cheap**.
Die graue Schirmmütze ist billig.

● Bei ungleichen Dingen hängst du **-er** an das Adjektiv an und benutzt **than**:

The blue cap is **cheaper than** the grey cap.
Die blaue Schirmmütze ist billiger als die graue.

● Bei dem „Spitzenreiter" einer Gruppe hängst du **-est** an das Adjektiv an:

The white cap is the **cheapest**.
Die weiße Schirmmütze ist die billigste / am billigsten.

● Sind zwei Dinge gleich, benutzt du **as ... as**:

The black cap is **as cheap as** the blue cap.
Die schwarze Schirmmütze ist so billig wie die blaue.

● Achtung! Bei manchen Adjektiven ändert sich die Schreibweise:

nice	nic**er**	nic**est**
pretty	prett**ier**	prett**iest**
big	big**ger**	big**gest**

● **good** und **bad** haben unregelmäßige Vergleichsformen:

good	**better**	**best**
bad	**worse**	**worst**

tip:
In Theme 4 lernst du, Dinge zu vergleichen:
Hier ein Spiel, mit dem ihr üben könnt, Vergleichssätze zu bilden.
Denkt euch Beispielsätze aus und schreibt die Elemente auf einzelne
Blätter, z.B.

| My bike | is | newer | than | your bike |

Verteilt diese Blätter ungeordnet an eine 5er-Gruppe. Diese muss sich
schnell in der richtigen Reihenfolge aufstellen.

Is Charlie **taller** than Vera?

19 Vergleichsformen (2) – „more …, most …“

- Lange Adjektive (mit zwei oder mehr Silben) bilden die Vergleichsformen mit **more** und **most**:

The teddy earrings are **expensive**.
Die Teddy-Ohrringe sind teuer.

The snake earrings are **more expensive** than the teddy earrings.
Die Schlangen-Ohrringe sind teurer als die Teddy-Ohrringe.

The dinosaur earrings are the **most expensive**.
Die Dinosaurier-Ohrringe sind die teuersten / am teuersten.

20 „these“ – „those“

- **these** und **those** sind die Mehrzahlformen von **this** und **that**.
  Du benutzt sie, wenn du zwei Sachen oder Personen unterscheiden willst.

*These earrings are nice. But **those** earrings are fantastic.*

Diese Ohrringe (hier) sind schön. Aber die Ohrringe (da drüben) sind fantastisch.

21 „can, must, mustn't, have to"

● Mit **can** kannst du nicht nur sagen, was jemand kann, sondern auch, was jemand darf:

Can I wear these shorts tonight?

No, you **can't**.

Kann/Darf ich diese Shorts heute Abend tragen?   *Nein.*

● **must** klingt wie „muss" und es heißt auch „müssen":

Pupils **must** be polite.
Die Schülerinnen und Schüler müssen höflich sein.

Pupils **must** wear sports gear for sports.
Die Schülerinnen und Schüler müssen im Sportunterricht Sportkleidung tragen.

● Du kannst **must** auch durch **have to / has to** ersetzen. Es bedeutet dasselbe.

Gillian **must** do her homework before she can go out.
Gillian **has to** do her homework before she can go out.
Gillian muss ihre Hausaufgaben machen, bevor sie ausgehen darf.

● Vorsicht! **must not** oder die Kurzform **mustn't** klingt wie „muss nicht", aber es heißt „etwas nicht dürfen":

Pupils **must not** eat in the lessons.
Die Schülerinnen und Schüler dürfen im Unterricht nicht essen.

● Wenn du sagen willst, was jemand nicht tun muss, benutzt du **don't/doesn't have to**:

In our school we **don't have to** wear a school uniform.
In unserer Schule müssen wir keine Schuluniform tragen.

David **doesn't have to** eat the school dinner.
David muss das Schulessen nicht essen.

tip:
In Theme 5 lernst du zu sagen, was jemand darf, nicht darf oder tun muss.
Such dir ein Thema aus und versuche eigene Sätze mit **can, must** und **mustn't** aufzuschreiben, z. B.

<u>Rules for my room:</u>
Mum mustn't read my letters.
...

6

LiF

22 present perfect (1) – Die vollendete Gegenwart

● Du brauchst diese Zeitform für Handlungen oder Ereignisse, die in der Vergangenheit angefangen haben und noch nicht zu Ende sind:

He **has been** in this tree for eighteen hours.
Er ist schon seit achtzehn Stunden in diesem Baum.

● Du benutzt diese Form auch, wenn die Handlungen oder Ereignisse schon beendet sind, aber noch in die Gegenwart hineinwirken:

 I **have caught** a terrible cold.

Ich habe mir eine schreckliche Erkältung geholt.

● Du nimmst das *present perfect* auch, wenn du sagen willst, was jemand schon einmal, häufig oder noch nie getan hat:

He **has** never **been** to the Rockies before.
Er ist noch nie zuvor in den Rockies gewesen.

23 Present Perfect (2) – Das Partizip

● Das *present perfect* besteht aus zwei Teilen:

have/has + **Partizip (3. Verbform)**

	have/has	Partizip	
I	have	caught	a cold.
You	have	met	a reporter.
He/she/it	has	watched	a grizzly.
We	have	found	the man.
You	have	visited	many countries.
They	have	been	here before.

● Auch beim *present perfect* gibt es Kurzformen:

I**'ve**
You**'ve**
He**'s**
She**'s**   **caught** a cold.
It**'s**
We**'ve**
You**'ve**
They**'ve**

a) Regelmäßige Verben bilden das Partizip mit **-ed**.

Infinitiv (1. Form)	*simple past* (2. Form)	Partizip (3. Form)
clean	clean**ed**	clean**ed**
play	play**ed**	play**ed**
visit	visit**ed**	visit**ed**
watch	watch**ed**	watch**ed**
try	tri**ed**	tri**ed**
…	…	…

b) Unregelmäßige Verben haben auch ein unregelmäßiges Partizip.

Infinitiv (1. Form)	*simple past* (2. Form)	Partizip (3. Form)
be	was/were	been
do	did	done
have	had	had
buy	bought	bought
catch	caught	caught
find	found	found
keep	kept	kept
lose	lost	lost
meet	met	met
read	read	read

24 Present Perfect (3) – Ja/Nein-Fragen

● Bei Ja/Nein-Fragen steht **have** oder **has** am Satzanfang.

Have you ever **talked** to a hippo?
Hast du jemals mit einem Nilpferd gesprochen?

Yes, I **have**. / **No**, I **haven't**.
Ja.   / Nein.

Has Charlie ever **been** to Germany?
Ist Charlie jemals in Deutschland gewesen?

Yes, he **has**. / **No**, he **hasn't**.
Ja.   / Nein.

tip:
Welcher der bisher genannten Grammatik-Lerntipps gefällt dir am besten, um das *present perfect* zu üben? Wähle eine Möglichkeit, probiere sie aus und stelle sie der Klasse vor!

Vokabelanhang

Die Wortlisten nach Kapiteln

Hier sind alle neuen Wörter in der Reihenfolge aufgelistet, wie sie vorne im Buch auftauchen. In der linken Spalte ist das englische Wort mit der dazugehörigen Lautschrift. Sie zeigt an, wie man das Wort ausspricht. Dies wird auf der nächsten Seite genauer erklärt.

In der mittleren Spalte steht die deutsche Entsprechung für das englische Wort und in der rechten Spalte sind oft Beispielsätze oder kleine Bildchen, die dir dabei helfen, dir Wörter besser einzuprägen.

Alle fett gedruckten Wörter solltest du dir merken.

Alle Wörter mit einem Sternchen * gehören zu Texten, die zusätzlich angeboten werden. Sie sind kein Lernwortschatz.

In den Lerntipps stehen Vorschläge, wie du am besten mit den neuen Wörtern umgehst.

Die alphabetischen Wortlisten

Wenn du nicht mehr weißt, wo ein Wort zum ersten Mal aufgetaucht ist (und es nicht findest), kannst du es in der alphabetischen Wortliste ab **Seite 129** nachschlagen. Und auf der nächsten Seite kannst du dir noch einmal das englische Alphabet ansehen.

Wendungen, die aus mehreren Wörtern bestehen, kannst du auch in der alphabetischen Wortliste nachschlagen. Sie sind meistens unter verschiedenen Stichwörtern einsortiert, z.B. *at home* steht sowohl unter *at* als auch unter *home*.

Wenn du mal eine Aufgabe machst, bei der du ein englisches Wort brauchst, das du nicht kennst, kannst du in der deutsch-englischen Wortliste ab **Seite 141** nachsehen. Falls du das benötigte Wort dort nicht findest, überlege, ob es nicht ein ähnliches deutsches Wort gibt, das in dieser Liste steht. Sonst bleibt dir noch der Griff zum Wörterbuch.

Die englische Lautschrift

Im Englischen spricht man Wörter oft anders aus, als man sie schreibt.

Das ist aber kein Problem. Denn die Aussprache der Wörter ist in jedem Wörterbuch angegeben. So kann man auch neue Wörter richtig aussprechen, ohne sie vorher gehört zu haben.

Dazu nimmt man die so genannte Lautschrift zu Hilfe. Das ist eine Schrift, deren Symbole jeden Laut genau bezeichnen. Die Lautschrift wird in jedem Wörterbuch benutzt.

Hier ist eine Liste mit den Symbolen dieser Lautschrift zusammen mit Beispielwörtern, in denen der entsprechende Laut vorkommt.

Vokale

[ɑ:] **a**rm
[ʌ] b**u**t
[e] d**e**sk
[ə] th**e**, **a**n
[ɜ:] g**ir**l, b**ir**d
[æ] **a**pple
[ɪ] **i**n, **i**t
[i:] **ea**sy, **ea**t
[ɒ] **o**range, s**o**rry
[ɔ:] **a**ll, c**a**ll
[ʊ] l**oo**k
[u:] b**oo**t

Doppellaute

[aɪ] **eye**, b**y**, b**uy**
[aʊ] **ou**r
[eə] **ai**r, th**ere**
[eɪ] t**a**ke, th**ey**
[ɪə] h**ere**
[ɔɪ] b**oy**
[əʊ] g**o**, **o**ld
[ʊə] y**ou're**

Konsonanten

[ŋ] so**ng**, lo**ng**
[r] **r**ed, **r**ight
[s] **s**i**s**ter, cla**ss** (scharfes s)
[z] no**s**e, dog**s** (weiches s)
[ʒ] televi**si**on
[dʒ] sausa**ge**
[ʃ] fre**sh**
[tʃ] **ch**ild, **ch**eese
[ð] **th**ese, mo**th**er (weicher Laut)
[θ] ba**th**room, **th**ink (harter Laut)
[v] **v**ery, ha**v**e
[w] **wh**at, **w**ord

[ˈ] Betonungszeichen für die folgende Silbe (Hauptbetonung)
[ˌ] Betonungszeichen für die folgende Silbe (Nebenbetonung)
[:] langer Vokal

Das englische Alphabet

a	[eɪ]	h	[eɪtʃ]	o	[əʊ]	v	[vi:]
b	[bi:]	i	[aɪ]	p	[pi:]	w	[ˈdʌblju:]
c	[si:]	j	[dʒeɪ]	q	[kju:]	x	[eks]
d	[di:]	k	[keɪ]	r	[ɑ:]	y	[waɪ]
e	[i:]	l	[el]	s	[es]	z	[zed]
f	[ef]	m	[em]	t	[ti:]		
g	[dʒi:]	n	[en]	u	[ju:]		

A1

after [ˈɑːftə]	nach
holiday [ˈhɒlədeɪ]	Ferien, Urlaub
these [ðiːz]	diese (Mz)
photo [ˈfəʊtəʊ]	Foto
really [ˈrɪəlɪ]	wirklich
just [dʒʌst]	nur, gerade, einfach
live [lɪv]	leben, wohnen
there [ðeə]	da(hin), dort(hin)
out of [ˈaʊt̬ əv]	aus ... heraus
look after [ˌlʊk̬ ˈɑːftə]	sich kümmern um
stable [ˈsteɪbl]	Stall
forget [fəˈget]	vergessen
stay [steɪ]	bleiben, sich aufhalten
have a good time [ˌhæv̬ ə gʊd ˈtaɪm]	sich vergnügen
visit [ˈvɪzɪt]	besuchen

A4

place [pleɪs]	Ort, Platz
much [mʌtʃ]	viel, sehr
rain [reɪn]	Regen
like [laɪk]	(so) wie
Love [lʌv]	Herzliche Grüße (Briefschluss)

weather [ˈweðə]	Wetter
beach [biːtʃ]	Strand
apartment [əˈpɑːtmənt]	Wohnung
so [səʊ]	also, daher
everything [ˈevrɪθɪŋ]	alles
building [ˈbɪldɪŋ]	Gebäude
yesterday [ˈjestədeɪ]	gestern
boat [bəʊt]	Boot
trip [trɪp]	Ausflug
around [əˈraʊnd]	um ... herum
soon [suːn]	bald
bone [bəʊn]	Knochen
dry [draɪ]	trocken
sunny [ˈsʌnɪ]	sonnig
friendly [ˈfrendlɪ]	freundlich
country [ˈkʌntrɪ]	Land
sight [saɪt]	Sehenswürdigkeit
other [ˈʌðə]	andere(r, s)
everyone [ˈevrɪwʌn]	jede/r
near [nɪə]	nahe, in der Nähe (von)
castle [kɑːsl]	Schloss
way [weɪ]	Weg
south [saʊθ]	Süden
good-looking [ˌgʊd ˈlʊkɪŋ]	gut aussehend

A5

summer [ˈsʌmə]	Sommer
festival [ˈfestəvl]	Feier, Festival
some [sʌm]	einige, etwas
lie [laɪ]	liegen
sun [sʌn]	Sonne
land [lænd]	landen
sea [siː]	Meer
empty [ˈemptɪ]	leer
can [kæn]	Dose
enjoy [ɪnˈdʒɔɪ]	genießen
somewhere [ˈsʌmweə]	irgendwo

 before the holidays  after the holidays

Don't forget your camera.
Susan stayed at home.

 There's not much milk.

yesterday   today   tomorrow

The house is near the park.

summer ≠ winter

There are some trees in the park.

A6	at first [ət 'fɜːst]	zuerst
	end [end]	Ende
	warm [wɔːm]	warm
	wet [wet]	nass
	windy ['wɪndɪ]	windig
	cloudy ['klaʊdɪ]	wolkig, bewölkt
	foggy ['fɒgɪ]	neblig
	no [nəʊ]	kein(e)
	fog [fɒg]	Nebel
B1	**race** [reɪs]	Rennen
	riding lesson ['raɪdɪŋ ˌlesn]	Reitstunde
B2	fun [fʌn]	Spaß
	commentator ['kɒmənteɪtə]	Berichterstatter
	rider ['raɪdər]	Reiter
	off [ɒf]	weg, fort, los
	in front [ɪn 'frʌnt]	vorn
	Oh dear (me)! [ˌəʊ 'dɪə (miː)]	Ach je!, Du liebe Zeit!
	hungry ['hʌŋgrɪ]	hungrig
	Wait a minute! ['weɪt‿ə ˌmɪnɪt]	Moment mal!
	both [bəʊθ]	beide
	jump [dʒʌmp]	(über)springen
	hedge [hedʒ]	Hecke
	racecourse ['reɪskɔːs]	Rennbahn
	turn (around) [ˌtɜːn (ə'raʊnd)]	sich (um)drehen
	finishing line ['fɪnɪʃɪŋ laɪn]	Ziellinie
	Well done! [ˌwel 'dʌn]	Gut gemacht!
B4	sunflower ['sʌnflaʊə]	Sonnenblume
	cross [krɒs]	überqueren
B6	**hotel** [həʊ'tel]	Hotel
	bad [bæd]	schlecht, schlimm
	terrible ['terəbl]	schrecklich
	camp site ['kæmp saɪt]	Campingplatz
	cycle ['saɪkl]	Rad fahren
B7	**together** [tə'geðə]	zusammen
	until [ʌn'tɪl]	bis
C1	science ['saɪəns]	Naturwissenschaft
	letter ['letə]	Brief
	wish [wɪʃ]	wünschen
	why [waɪ]	warum
	the same [ðə 'seɪm]	der/die/das gleiche
	as [æz, əz]	wie (Vergleich)
	move [muːv]	(sich) bewegen
	month [mʌnθ]	Monat
	at the top [ət ðə 'tɒp]	oben
	hate [heɪt]	hassen
	smell (of) [smel (əv)]	riechen, duften, stinken (nach)
	love [lʌv]	lieben
	think about ['θɪŋk‿əˌbaʊt]	nachdenken über, denken an
C2	**calculator** ['kælkjəleɪtə]	Taschenrechner
	mouse (Mz: mice) [maʊs, maɪs]	Maus
	map [mæp]	Stadtplan, Landkarte
	Bunsen burner [ˌbʌnsn 'bɜːnə]	Bunsenbrenner
	pupil ['pjuːpl]	Schüler/in

wet ≠ dry

No dogs in the park!

This is Peter and that is Paul. They are both 13.

good ≠ bad

Peter and Paul are good friends. They do everything together.

Why are you late?

There are twelve months in a year.

WORDS

	ruler ['ruːlə]	Lineal
	smoke [sməʊk]	Rauch
	eraser [ɪ'reɪzə]	Radiergummi
	envelope ['envələʊp]	(Brief)Umschlag
	magazine [ˌmægə'ziːn]	Zeitschrift
C3	**round** [raʊnd]	rund
	square [skweə]	eckig, quadratisch
	soft [sɒft]	weich
	hard [hɑːd]	hart, schwierig
	at the back [ət ðə 'bæk]	hinten
	at the front [ət ðə 'frʌnt]	vorn
	in the middle [ɪn ðə 'mɪdl]	in der Mitte
C4	**quarter (to/past)** ['kwɔːtə]	Viertel (vor/nach)
	end [end]	aufhören, enden
	half [hɑːf]	halb
	past [pɑːst]	nach
	which [wɪtʃ]	welche(r, s)
	enough [ɪ'nʌf]	genug
	early ['ɜːlɪ]	früh
C5	*chant [tʃɑːnt]	Sprechgesang, Rap
	*felt tip [ˌfel'tɪp]	Filzstift
	*paper clip ['peɪpə klɪp]	Büroklammer
	*glue [gluː]	Klebstoff, Leim
	*bag [bæg]	Tasche, Beutel
	*full [fʊl]	voll
	*pencil case ['pensl ˌkeɪs]	Federmäppchen

a hard chair   a hard test
hard ≠ soft   hard ≠ difficult

Do we have enough food for the weekend?

Lerntipp

WÖRTER SAMMELN
Sicher habt ihr in der Klasse besprochen, wie ihr eure Englisch-Unterlagen organisieren könnt.
Vokabel-Ordner:
Dein persönlicher Ordner hat nämlich den Vorteil, dass du immer wieder Seiten dazwischenheften kannst. Die Seiten kannst du mit Zeichnungen oder Fotos bunt gestalten – ganz nach deinem Geschmack.
Vokabel-Kartei:
Schreibe einzelne Vokabeln auf Kärtchen – auf der einen Seite auf Deutsch, auf der anderen Seite auf Englisch. Du kannst die Wörter mal Englisch-Deutsch und mal Deutsch-Englisch üben.

Wortfeld

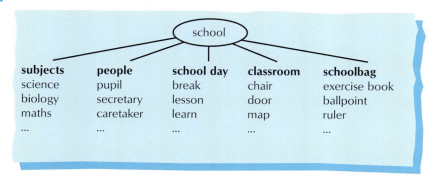

subjects	**people**	**school day**	**classroom**	**schoolbag**
science	pupil	break	chair	exercise book
biology	secretary	lesson	door	ballpoint
maths	caretaker	learn	map	ruler
...	...	...	...	...

A1	**tiger** [ˈtaɪgə]	Tiger
	sleepy [ˈsliːpɪ]	schläfrig
	cage [keɪdʒ]	Käfig
	clever [ˈklevə]	klug, schlau
	stripe [straɪp]	Streifen
	zoo [zuː]	Zoo
	slow [sləʊ]	langsam
	wild [waɪld]	wild
	dangerous [ˈdeɪndʒərəs]	gefährlich
A2	**alone** [əˈləʊn]	allein
	news [njuːz]	Nachrichten
	be frightened [bɪ ˈfraɪtnd]	Angst haben
	newsreader [ˈnjuːzˌriːdə]	Nachrichtensprecher/in
	keeper [ˈkiːpə]	Wärter/in
	help [help]	Hilfe
	meal [miːl]	Mahlzeit
	someone [ˈsʌmwʌn]	jemand
	garden [ˈgɑːdn]	Garten
	What's the matter? [ˌwɒts ðə ˈmætə]	Was ist los?
	close [kləʊz]	zumachen, schließen
	latest [ˈleɪtɪst]	neueste(r, s)
	try [traɪ]	versuchen
	catch [kætʃ]	fangen
	Thank goodness! [ˌθæŋk ˈgʊdnəs]	Gott sei Dank!
A3	**hamster** [ˈhæmstə]	Hamster
	meat [miːt]	Fleisch
	horse [hɔːs]	Pferd
	elephant [ˈelɪfənt]	Elefant
	sea lion [ˈsiː ˌlaɪən]	Seelöwe
	plant [plɑːnt]	Pflanze
	crocodile [ˈkrɒkədaɪl]	Krokodil
	grass [grɑːs]	Gras
	snake [sneɪk]	Schlange
A4	polar bear [ˈpəʊlə ˌbeə]	Eisbär
	*into [ˈɪntə]	in, in ... hinein
	*giraffe [dʒəˈrɑːf]	Giraffe
A5	**usually** [ˈjuːʒʊəlɪ]	gewöhnlich, normalerweise
	hole [həʊl]	Loch
	aquarium [əˈkweərɪəm]	Aquarium
	chimpanzee [ˌtʃɪmpənˈziː]	Schimpanse
	field [fiːld]	Feld
	fly [flaɪ]	fliegen
A6	dolphin [ˈdɒlfɪn]	Delfin
	peaceful [ˈpiːsfʊl]	friedlich
	than [ðæn, ðən]	als (bei Vergleichen)
B1	**them** [ðem]	sie (Mz), ihnen
	tube [tjuːb]	U-Bahn (in London)
	well [wel]	tja, nun, also
	to [tuː, tʊ]	vor (Uhrzeit)
	beautiful [ˈbjuːtəfʊl]	schön
	be lucky [bɪ ˈlʌkɪ]	Glück haben
	that [ðæt, ðət]	dass
	away [əˈweɪ]	weg, fort
	later [ˈleɪtə]	später

slow ≠ fast

He is frightened of mice.

Breakfast, lunch and dinner are meals.

Close the door, please!

catch a ball

David usually goes to Wales in the summer holidays.

Birds can fly.

Gillian can take the tube or the bus to Hendon.

See you later!

sure [ʃʊə]   sicher
B3 sharp [ʃɑːp]   scharf
(5) pm [ˌpiː ˈem]   (5 Uhr) nachmittags, abends

fur [fɜː]   Fell, Pelz
tusk [tʌsk]   Stoßzahn
trunk [trʌŋk]   Rüssel
bath [bɑːθ]   Bad
flamingo [fləˈmɪŋgəʊ]   Flamingo
lion [ˈlaɪən]   Löwe
light [laɪt]   hell-
hippopotamus (hippo) [ˌhɪpəˈpɒtəməs (ˈhɪpəʊ)]   Nilpferd
mouth [maʊθ]   Mund, Maul
flipper [ˈflɪpə]   Flosse
because [bɪˈkɒz]   weil

funny [ˈfʌnɪ]   lustig, komisch
cuddly [ˈkʌdlɪ]   kuschlig
B4 *striped [straɪpt]   gestreift
* bite [baɪt]   beißen
* fat [fæt]   dick, fett
* thin [θɪn]   dünn
* hairy [ˈheərɪ]   haarig
* bark [bɑːk]   bellen
* night [naɪt]   Nacht, Abend
* awake [əˈweɪk]   wach
* asleep [əˈsliːp]   schlafend
* blind [blaɪnd]   Blinde/r
* sheep [ʃiːp]   Schaf(e)
* everywhere [ˈevrɪweə]   überall(hin)
* chase [tʃeɪs]   jagen
* rat [ræt]   Ratte
* giraffe [dʒəˈrɑːf]   Giraffe
* ever [ˈevə]   jemals
* woolly [ˈwʊlɪ]   wollig
* scarf (Mz: scarves) [skɑːf (skɑːvz)]   Schal
* neck [nek]   Hals
* ground [graʊnd]   Boden
B5 *when [wen]   als, wenn
* open [ˈəʊpən]   öffnen
* modern [ˈmɒdən]   modern
* home country [ˌhəʊm ˈkʌntrɪ]   Heimatland
* hut [hʌt]   Hütte
* African [ˈæfrɪkən]   afrikanisch
* for example [fərˌɪgˈzɑːmpl]   zum Beispiel
* born [bɔːn]   geboren
* rare [reə]   selten, rar
* giant [ˈdʒaɪənt]   Riesen-
* panda [ˈpændə]   Panda
* Asian [ˈeɪʃn]   asiatisch, Asiate/Asiatin
* money [ˈmʌnɪ]   Geld
* problem [ˈprɒbləm]   Problem
* adopt [əˈdɒpt]   adoptieren
* guinea pig [ˈgɪnɪ pɪg]   Meerschweinchen
* gecko [ˈgekəʊ]   Gecko

He is eating two hamburgers because he is very hungry.

	* also ['ɔ:lsəʊ]	auch
	* share [ʃeə]	teilen
	* giraffe [dʒəˈrɑːf]	Giraffe
	* hay [heɪ]	Heu
	* salt [sɔːlt]	Salz
	* wash down [ˌwɒʃ ˈdaʊn]	hinunterspülen
	* litre ['li:tə]	Liter
C1	kid [kɪd]	Kind
	queen [kwi:n]	Königin
	shop [ʃɒp]	Geschäft
	toy [tɔɪ]	Spielzeug
	juggler ['dʒʌglə]	Jongleur/in
	Londoner ['lʌndənə]	Londoner/in
	tourist ['tʊərɪst]	Tourist/in
	relax [rɪˈlæks]	sich entspannen
	speaker ['spi:kə]	Sprecher/in
	model [mɒdl]	Modell
	ship [ʃɪp]	Schiff
	plane [pleɪn]	Flugzeug
	also ['ɔ:lsəʊ]	auch
	modern ['mɒdən]	modern
	Japanese [ˌdʒæpəˈni:z]	japanisch
	doll [dɒl]	Puppe
	(8) am [(eɪt) ˌeɪ ˈem]	(8 Uhr) morgens, vor-mittags
	locomotive ['ləʊkəˈməʊtɪv]	Lokomotive
	famous ['feɪməs]	berühmt
	world [wɜːld]	Welt
	wax [wæks]	Wachs
	king [kɪŋ]	König
	sportsperson ['spɔːtsˌpɜːsn]	Sportler/in
	even ['i:vn]	sogar
	mean [mi:n]	bedeuten, meinen
	adventure [ədˈventʃə]	Abenteuer
	star [stɑː]	Stern
	moon [mu:n]	Mond
	European [ˌjʊərəˈpi:ən]	europäisch
	more [mɔː]	mehr
	midnight ['mɪdnaɪt]	Mitternacht
	bridge [brɪdʒ]	Brücke
	open up [ˌəʊpən ˈʌp]	aufmachen, sich öffnen
	large [lɑːdʒ]	groß
	pass [pɑːs]	vorbeigehen, *hier:* durch-fahren
	several ['sevrəl]	mehrere, einige
	tower ['taʊə]	Turm
	cannon ['kænən]	Kanone
	uniform ['juːnɪfɔːm]	Uniform
	past [pɑːst]	Vergangenheit
	bear [beə]	Bär
	snail [sneɪl]	Schnecke
	spider ['spaɪdə]	Spinne
	shark [ʃɑːk]	Hai
	about [əˈbaʊt]	ungefähr
C2	rainy ['reɪnɪ]	regnerisch
	money ['mʌnɪ]	Geld
	bus [bʌs]	Bus

Superstore is a shop in Hendon.

He collects model planes.

He also collects stamps.

Sherlock Holmes was a famous detective.

This means: No dogs!

Can I have more chocolate, please?

large ≠ small

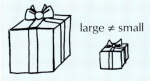

How tall is your sister?

About 1 m.

C4	**spend** [spend]	verbringen
	afterwards [ˈɑːftəwədz]	danach
C5	**guided tour** [ˌgaɪdɪd ˈtʊə]	Führung
	visitor [ˈvɪzɪtə]	Besucher/in

> We had lunch first. Afterwards we went to the zoo.

Lerntipps

WORTBILDER
Schau dir einmal die Abbildungen der Wörter *sunny, windy, foggy* auf S. 19 an. Vielleicht kannst du dir Vokabeln besser merken, wenn du daraus solche „Wortbilder" machst. Versuche es mal selbst mit den Wörtern *grass, plant, fast, slow* oder mit Tiernamen. Wer kann das interessanteste oder lustigste Wortbild erfinden?

WORTFELDER
Wenn man Wörter, die zusammengehören, auch zusammen lernt, kann man sie sich besser merken. In Theme 1 hast du z.B. weitere Wörter rund ums Thema *school* kennen gelernt, in Theme 2 viele *pets and animals*. Stelle sie zu Wortfeldern zusammen (wie S. 114) und sammle sie in deinem Vokabelordner. Wenn später noch mehr Wörter dazukommen, trägst du sie einfach nach. Deine Wortfelder werden dann immer größer.

WORTNETZE
Wortfelder kannst du auch in „Wortnetzen" *(mindmaps)* zusammenstellen. Sieh dir mal das Wortnetz zum Thema *nature* an. Verzweigungen entstehen, wenn du Wörter so zuordnest, wie sie für dich logisch zusammenpassen.

Wortnetz

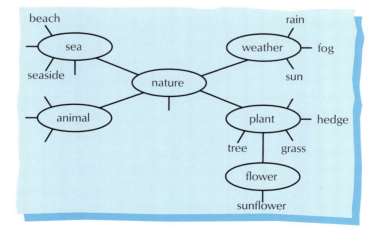

Over to you. [ˌəʊvə tʊ ˈjuː] Weiter mit dir/euch!

A1 hero (Mz: heroes) [ˈhɪərəʊ (ˈhɪərəʊz)] Held

read [riːd] lesen
dream [driːm] träumen
will [wɪl] werden *(Zukunft)*
grow up [ˌɡrəʊˈʌp] erwachsen werden, groß werden

David reads a lot of comics and magazines.

I'll (= I will) [aɪl] ich werde
trek [trek] Treck, Reise
cattle [ˈkætl] Vieh
astronaut [ˈæstrənɔːt] Astronaut
bow [bəʊ] Bogen
arrow [ˈærəʊ] Pfeil
ask for [ˈɑːsk fɔː] bitten um
sportsman [ˈspɔːtsmən] Sportler

A2 pilot [ˈpaɪlət] Pilot/in

A3 vet [vet] Tierarzt, Tierärztin
fairy tale [ˈfeərɪ ˌteɪl] Märchen
horror story [ˈhɒrə ˌstɔːrɪ] Gruselgeschichte
person [ˈpɜːsn] Person
strong [strɒŋ] stark

Can we have an ice-cream?

The children are asking for an ice-cream.

strong

A4 **know** [nəʊ] wissen, kennen
once [wʌns] einmal, einst
put on [ˌpʊtˈɒn] anziehen
(2 minutes) ago [(tʊ ˌmɪnɪts) əˈɡəʊ] vor (2 Minuten)

Gillian is putting on her red jacket.

follow [ˈfɒləʊ] folgen
hang [hæŋ] hängen
hope [həʊp] hoffen
get to [ˈɡet tʊ] *hier:* hinkommen
oak [əʊk] Eiche
at last [ət ˈlɑːst] endlich
a few [ə ˈfjuː] ein paar
hat [hæt] Hut, Kopfbedeckung
this time [ˈðɪs taɪm] dieses Mal
next time [ˈnekst taɪm] das nächste Mal
remember [rɪˈmembə] (sich) erinnern, denken an

a lot of books ≠ a few books

forest [ˈfɒrɪst] Wald
careful [ˈkeəfʊl] vorsichtig, behutsam

A5 **little** [lɪtl] klein

remember ≠ forget
I can remember the story of Robin Hood.

little = small
Sharon is Charlie's little sister.

kill [kɪl] umbringen
wolf (Mz: wolves) [wʊlf (wʊlvz)] Wolf
nose [nəʊz] Nase
glasses *(Mz)* [ˈɡlɑːsɪz] Brille

B1 **Ready, steady, go!** [ˌredɪ ˌstedɪ ˈɡəʊ] Achtung, fertig, los!
second [ˈsekənd] Sekunde
topic [ˈtɒpɪk] Thema
ice [aɪs] Eis
ice-skating [ˈaɪsˌskeɪtɪŋ] Schlittschuhlaufen
snowman [ˈsnəʊmæn] Schneemann
glove [ɡlʌv] Handschuh
scarf (Mz: scarves) [skɑːf (skɑːvz)] Schal

At some schools, the pupils wear school scarves.

	boot [buːt]	Stiefel
	woolly ['wʊlɪ]	wollig
	vest [vest]	Unterhemd
	Time's up. [ˌtaɪmz_'ʌp]	Die Zeit ist um.
	point [pɔɪnt]	Punkt
B3	**year 8** [ˌjɪə'r_eɪt]	6. Klasse
	shy [ʃaɪ]	schüchtern
	be good at [ˌbɪ 'gʊd_ət]	gut sein in/bei
	information technology [ˌɪnfə'meɪʃn tek'nɒlədʒɪ]	Informatik
	history ['hɪstrɪ]	Geschichte
	surf the internet [ˌsɜːf ðɪ 'ɪntənet]	im Internet surfen
	quite [kwaɪt]	ziemlich
	when [wen]	als, wenn
	answer ['ɑːnsə]	(be)antworten
	light [laɪt]	Licht, Lampe
	proud [praʊd]	stolz
B4	art [ɑːt]	Kunst
B5	semi-final [ˌsemi'faɪnl]	Halbfinale
	I hope so. [aɪ 'həʊp səʊ]	Das hoffe ich.
	lose [luːz]	verlieren
	won't (= will not) [wəʊnt]	nicht werden *(Zukunft)*
	championship ['tʃæmpjənʃɪp]	Meisterschaft
	a little [ə 'lɪtl]	ein bisschen, ein wenig
	talker ['tɔːkə]	Redner/in
	fine [faɪn]	fein, gut
	worried ['wʌrɪd]	besorgt, beunruhigt
	not at all [ˌnɒt_ə't_ɔːl]	überhaupt nicht
	squeeze [skwiːz]	drücken
	Good luck. [ˌgʊd 'lʌk]	Viel Glück!
C2	busker ['bʌskə]	Straßenmusikant/in
	guitar [gɪ'tɑː]	Gitarre
	comb [kəʊm]	Kamm
	paper ['peɪpə]	Papier
	crazy ['kreɪzɪ]	verrückt
	many ['menɪ]	viele
	one day [wʌn 'deɪ]	eines Tages
	pocket money ['pɒkɪt ˌmʌnɪ]	Taschengeld
	left [left]	übrig
	any ['enɪ]	irgendwelche, irgendein(e)
	hour ['aʊə]	Stunde
	get ready [ˌget 'redɪ]	sich fertig machen
	Off you go! [ˌɒf jʊ 'gəʊ]	Fort mit dir/euch!
	over ['əʊvə]	über
C4	**babysit** ['beɪbɪsɪt]	babysitten
	do a paper round [ˌduː_ə 'peɪpə raʊnd]	Zeitungen austragen
	repair [rɪ'peə]	reparieren
	take for a walk [ˌteɪk fər_ə 'wɔːk]	ausführen
	water ['wɔːtə]	gießen
C5	*musical instrument [ˌmjuːzɪkl 'ɪnstrʊmənt]	Musikinstrument
	* instrument ['ɪnstrʊmənt]	Instrument
	* clap [klæp]	klatschen

He's not very good at maths.

This T-shirt is quite nice, but that T-shirt is very nice.

win ≠ lose

a little milk ≠ a lot of milk

I have many friends.

How much pocket money do you get?

I sometimes get over £5.

She is taking her children for a walk.

* spoon [spuːn] — Löffel
* sit down [ˌsɪt 'daʊn] — sich hinsetzen
* hold [həʊld] — halten
* back-to-back [ˌbæk tə 'bæk] — mit der Rückseite zueinander
* index finger ['ɪndeks ˌfɪŋgə] — Zeigefinger
* tightly ['taɪtlɪ] — fest, eng
* hit [hɪt] — treffen, schlagen
* own [əʊn] — eigene(r, s)
* rhythm ['rɪðəm] — Rhythmus
* shaker ['ʃeɪkə] — Shaker, Mixbecher
* rice [raɪs] — Reis
* elastic band [ɪˌlæstɪk 'bænd] — Gummiband
* fill [fɪl] — füllen
* cover ['kʌvə] — bedecken
* opening ['əʊpnɪŋ] — Öffnung
* shake [ʃeɪk] — schütteln
* trumpet ['trʌmpɪt] — Trompete
* blow (up) [ˌbləʊ_('ʌp)] — (auf)blasen
* closed [kləʊzd] — geschlossen
* thumb [θʌm] — Daumen
* pull apart [ˌpʊl_ə'pɑːt] — auseinander ziehen
* finger ['fɪŋgə] — Finger
* stretch [stretʃ] — dehnen
* sound [saʊnd] — klingen
* air [eə] — Luft
* change [tʃeɪndʒ] — (sich) verändern
* fold [fəʊld] — falten
* tooth (Mz: teeth) [tuːθ (tiːθ)] — Zahn
* onto ['ɒntuː] — auf

C6 * hear [hɪə] — hören
* break of day [ˌbreɪk_əv 'deɪ] — Tagesanbruch
* chorus ['kɔːrəs] — Chor
* get late [ˌget 'leɪt] — spät werden

Lerntipp

VERGISS ES EINFACH!
Hast du manchmal Probleme, dir bestimmte Wörter zu merken? Sind es immer wieder dieselben Vokabeln, die dir nicht einfallen wollen? Dann probier es doch einfach mal mit Vergessen!
Das geht so: Suche fünf oder sechs solcher schwierigen Wörter aus, die du unbedingt vergessen willst. Schreibe sie auf einen oder mehrere Zettel. Hänge die Zettel neben dein Bett, über deinen Schreibtisch oder an den Badezimmerspiegel. Lies sie bei jeder Gelegenheit durch, damit du dich daran erinnerst, welche Wörter du unbedingt vergessen willst.

Wortfeld

Jobs

pilot	singer	secretary
vet	queen	caretaker
boxer	commentator	busker
filmstar	newsreader	juggler
stuntman	teacher	...

A1
high street ['haɪ striːt]	Haupt-/Einkaufsstraße
let off [ˌlet ˈɒf]	*hier:* abfeuern
fireworks ['faɪəˌwɜːks]	Feuerwerk
wish [wɪʃ]	Wunsch
church [tʃɜːtʃ]	Kirche
punch [pʌntʃ]	Punsch
decorate ['dekəreɪt]	dekorieren, schmücken
neighbour ['neɪbə]	Nachbar/in
Happy New Year! [ˌhæpɪ njuː ˈjɪə]	Frohes neues Jahr!
go for a walk [ˌgəʊ fərˌə ˈwɔːk]	einen Spaziergang machen

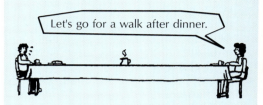

Let's go for a walk after dinner.

A2
New Year's Eve [ˌnjuː jɪəz ˈiːv]	Silvester
special ['speʃl]	besondere(r, s)
send [send]	senden, schicken

People in Britain send a lot of cards at Christmas.

card [kɑːd]	Karte
What time? [wɒt ˈtaɪm]	Um wie viel Uhr?

A3
New Year [ˌnjuː ˈjɪə]	Neujahr
Asian ['eɪʃn]	asiatisch, Asiate/Asiatin
most [məʊst]	die meisten, am meisten
celebrate ['selɪbreɪt]	feiern
twice [twaɪs]	zweimal
celebration [ˌselɪ'breɪʃn]	Feier
own [əʊn]	eigene(r, s)
Hindu ['hɪnduː]	Hindu
god [gɒd]	Gott
welcome ['welkəm]	willkommen heißen
goddess ['gɒdɪs]	Göttin
delicious [dɪ'lɪʃəs]	köstlich, lecker
recipe ['resɪpiː]	Rezept
page [peɪdʒ]	Seite
Muslim ['mʊslɪm]	Moslem/Moslime
different ['dɪfrənt]	verschieden
prophet ['prɒfɪt]	Prophet
city ['sɪtɪ]	(Groß)Stadt
*wholemeal ['həʊlmiːl]	Vollkorn-
*flour ['flaʊə]	Mehl
*salt [sɔːlt]	Salz
*teaspoon ['tiːspuːn]	Teelöffel
*tablespoon ['teɪblspuːn]	Esslöffel
*vegetable oil ['vedʒtəbl ˌɔɪl]	pflanzliches Öl
*bowl [bəʊl]	Schüssel
*add [æd]	hinzufügen
*mix [mɪks]	mixen, mischen
*well [wel]	gut
*knead [niːd]	kneten
*leave [liːv]	(be)lassen
*dough [dəʊ]	Teig
*form [fɔːm]	formen, bilden
*ball [bɔːl]	Kugel
*roll out [ˌrəʊlˌ'aʊt]	ausrollen
*rest [rest]	Rest
*flat [flæt]	flach, platt
*heat [hiːt]	erhitzen
*deep [diːp]	tief
*pan [pæn]	Pfanne

twice = 2x

The interview with Claire is on page 54.

Berlin and Cologne are German cities.

	* bake [beɪk]	backen
	candle ['kændl]	Kerze
	plan [plæn]	Plan
	beginning [bɪ'gɪnɪŋ]	Anfang
	lamp [læmp]	Lampe
	window ['wɪndəʊ]	Fenster
	string [strɪŋ]	Schnur, Kette
	coloured ['kʌləd]	farbig
	stereo ['sterɪəʊ]	Stereoanlage
	Indian ['ɪndjən]	indisch(e, er, es), Inder/in
	real [rɪəl]	wirklich, richtig
	sound [saʊnd]	Klang, Geräusch
	dance [dɑːns]	Tanz
A5	**glass** [glɑːs]	Glas
	bottle ['bɒtl]	Flasche
	full [fʊl]	voll
	stone [stəʊn]	Stein
B1	chocolates *(Mz)* ['tʃɒkləts]	Pralinen
	perfume ['pɜːfjuːm]	Parfüm
	handkerchief ['hæŋkətʃɪf]	Taschentuch
	writing paper ['raɪtɪŋ peɪpə]	Briefpapier
	goldfish ['gəʊldfɪʃ]	Goldfisch
	brilliant ['brɪljənt]	brillant, großartig
B2	**be out** [bɪ'aʊt]	unterwegs/draußen sein
	up and down [ˌʌp ən 'daʊn]	auf und ab
	shop window ['ʃɒp wɪndəʊ]	Schaufenster
	better ['betə]	besser
	expensive [ɪk'spensɪv]	teuer
	cheap [tʃiːp]	billig
	shall ['ʃæl]	soll
	department store	Kaufhaus
	[dɪ'pɑːtmənt ˌstɔː]	
	sunglasses ['sʌnglɑːsɪz]	Sonnenbrille
	handbag ['hændbæg]	Handtasche
	stationery ['steɪʃnərɪ]	Schreibwaren
	department [dɪ'pɑːtmənt]	Abteilung
	pretty ['prɪtɪ]	hübsch
	rose [rəʊz]	Rose
	needn't (= need not) ['niːdnt]	nicht brauchen, nicht müssen
B3	**What is/are ... like?**	Wie ist/sind ...?
	[ˌwɒt ɪz/ɑː 'laɪk]	
	as ... as [əz ... əz]	so ... wie
B4	**cauliflower** ['kɒlɪˌflaʊə]	Blumenkohl
	well [wel]	gut
	bake [beɪk]	backen
B5	**unusual** [ʌn'juːʒʊəl]	ungewöhnlich
	come round [ˌkʌm 'raʊnd]	vorbeischauen
	dress up [ˌdres 'ʌp]	sich verkleiden
	as [æz, əz]	als
	maid [meɪd]	Dienstmädchen
	lay the table [ˌleɪ ðə 'teɪbl]	den Tisch decken
	crown [kraʊn]	Krone
	into ['ɪntə]	in, in ... hinein
	serve [sɜːv]	servieren
	wonderful ['wʌndəfʊl]	wunderbar

Open the window, please!

an empty glass   a full glass

expensive ≠ cheap

A department store is a very big shop.

What's the weather like? It's warm and sunny.
What's Lisa like? She's very pretty.

The boy is coming out of the museum.
Two girls are going into the museum.

	polite [pə'laɪt]	höflich
	What a pity. [ˌwɒt_ə 'pɪtɪ]	Wie schade!
	a (year) [ə ('jɪə)]	pro (Jahr)
B6	**cook** [kʊk]	kochen
C1	strange [streɪndʒ]	seltsam, fremd
	raincoat ['reɪnkəʊt]	Regenmantel
	tomato (Mz: tomatoes) [tə'mɑːtəʊ (tə'mɑːtəʊz)]	Tomate
	fresh [freʃ]	frisch
	pick up [ˌpɪk_'ʌp]	(in die Hand) nehmen
	newspaper ['njuːspeɪpə]	Zeitung
	chemical ['kemɪkl]	Chemikalie
	walk up to [ˌwɔːk_'ʌp tə]	hingehen zu, sich nähern
	rainy season [ˌreɪnɪ 'siːzn]	Regenzeit
	umbrella [ʌm'brelə]	Regenschirm
	madam ['mædəm]	gnädige Frau (Anrede)
	open ['əʊpən]	öffnen
	bag [bæg]	Tasche, Beutel
	address [ə'dres]	Adresse
	may [meɪ]	dürfen
	keep [kiːp]	behalten, halten
	notice ['nəʊtɪs]	Notiz
C2	**could** [kʊd]	konnte, könnte
C3	**phone** [fəʊn]	anrufen
C4	**Christmas** ['krɪsməs]	Weihnachten
C6	*Lord [lɔːd]	Lord
	*part [pɑːt]	Teil
	*M'lord [mɪ'lɔːd]	Mein Herr (Anrede eines Lords)
	*surprised [sə'praɪzd]	überrascht
	*typical ['tɪpɪkl]	typisch
	*sir [sɜː]	Herr (förmliche Anrede)
	*cosmetics (Mz) [kɒz'metɪks]	Kosmetika
	*shirt [ʃɜːt]	Hemd
	*shirtmaker ['ʃɜːtmeɪkə]	Hemdenschneider/in
	*shoemaker ['ʃuːmeɪkə]	Schuhmacher/in
	*lipstick ['lɪpstɪk]	Lippenstift

Can you cook spaghetti?

adress

Oh Mum, can I keep the little cat?

Vera phones Gillian.

Lerntipp

GEGENSÄTZE
Neue Vokabeln musst du nicht immer in Listen schreiben. Du kannst sie auch anders sortieren, z.B. indem du Gegensätze zusammenstellst. Wie viele Wörter kennst du schon, die sich in dieser Weise zusammenstellen lassen?
Beispiele:

girl – boy	old – young
left – right	fast – slow
before – after	summer – winter
good – bad	...

Wortfeld

Food		Drinks	
hot	**cold**	**hot**	**cold**
meat	bread	coffee	juice
chips	carrot	hot chocolate	lemonade
egg	cheese	punch	milk
cauliflower	salad	tea	water
...	...	...	...

	dos and dont's [ˌduːz‿ən ˈdəʊnts]	Gebote und Verbote
A1	**problem** [ˈprɒbləm]	Problem
A2	**rule** [ruːl]	Regel
	penfriend [ˈpenfrend]	Brieffreund/in
	earring [ˈɪəˌrɪŋ]	Ohrring
	pink [pɪŋk]	rosa
	mustn't (= must not) [ˈmʌsnt]	nicht dürfen
	those [ðəʊz]	jene, die (da)
	silly [ˈsɪlɪ]	dumm, blöd
	have to [ˈhæv tə]	müssen
	stay up late [ˌsteɪ‿ʌp ˈleɪt]	lange aufbleiben
A3	**go out** [ˌgəʊ ˈaʊt]	ausgehen
	dye [daɪ]	färben
	cosmetics (Mz) [kɒzˈmetɪks]	Kosmetika
	sweets (Mz) [swiːts]	Süßigkeiten
A4	colourful [ˈkʌləfʊl]	farbig, bunt
A5	personal [ˈpɜːsnl]	persönlich
	taste [teɪst]	Geschmack
	geography [dʒɪˈɒgrəfɪ]	Erdkunde, Geographie
	technology [tekˈnɒlədʒɪ]	Technik, Technologie
	French [frentʃ]	Französisch
A6	record [ˈrekɔːd]	Rekord
	m (= metre) [ˈmiːtə]	Meter
	chewing gum [ˈtʃuːɪŋ ˌgʌm]	Kaugummi
	bubble [ˈbʌbl]	Blase
	cm (= centimetre) [ˈsentɪˌmiːtə]	Zentimeter
	ton [tʌn]	Tonne
	whale [weɪl]	Wal
	heavy [ˈhevɪ]	schwer
	kg (= kilogramme) [ˈkɪləgræm]	Kilogramm
	successful [səkˈsesfʊl]	erfolgreich
	malaria mosquito [məˈleərɪə məˌskiːtəʊ]	Malariamücke
B1	respect [rɪˈspekt]	respektieren, achten
	by [baɪ]	*hier:* bis
	who [huː]	der, die, das *(Relativpronomen)*
	deputy head [ˌdepjʊtɪ ˈhed]	Konrektor
	to [tuː, tʊ]	*hier:* bis
	shirt [ʃɜːt]	Hemd
	dark [dɑːk]	dunkel
	tie [taɪ]	Krawatte
	grey [greɪ]	grau
	trousers (Mz) [ˈtraʊzəz]	Hose(n)
	skirt [skɜːt]	Rock
	sports gear [ˈspɔːts ˌgɪə]	Sportkleidung
	smoke [sməʊk]	rauchen
	school grounds [ˈskuːl ˌgraʊndz]	Schulgelände
	school dinner [ˈskuːl ˌdɪnə]	Schulessen
	packed lunch [ˌpækt ˈlʌntʃ]	Lunchpaket
	diet [ˈdaɪət]	Diät
	note [nəʊt]	Notiz
	* mess about [ˌmes‿əˈbaʊt]	herumspielen
	* science lab [ˈsaɪəns ˌlæb]	Physiksaal
B3	**alarm clock** [əˈlɑːm ˌklɒk]	Wecker
	work [wɜːk]	funktionieren
	vegetarian [ˌvedʒɪˈteərɪən]	Vegetarier/in

We mustn't forget our homework.

these ≠ those
this ≠ that

Too many sweets are bad for you.

A pilot is a person who flies a plane.

Shirts, trousers and skirts are clothes.

B5	worse [wɜːs]	schlechter, schlimmer
C1	**safe** [seɪf]	sicher
	cycling ['saɪklɪŋ]	Radfahren
C2	keep on ['kiːp ˌɒn]	bleiben auf
	side [saɪd]	Seite
	carry ['kærɪ]	tragen, *hier:* mitnehmen
	passenger ['pæsɪndʒə]	Beifahrer/in, Mitfahrer/in
	seat [siːt]	Sitz
	hold on to [ˌhəʊld ˈɒn tʊ]	sich festhalten an
	handlebar ['hændlbɑː]	Lenkstange
	wheel [wiːl]	Rad
	saddle ['sædl]	Sattel
	low [ləʊ]	niedrig, tief
	helmet ['helmɪt]	Helm
	reflector [rɪ'flektə]	Rückstrahler
C3	*up [ʌp]	oben, hoch, hinauf
	* pedal ['pedl]	in die Pedale treten
	* down [daʊn]	unten, hinunter
	* Watch out! [ˌwɒtʃ ˈaʊt]	Pass auf!
C4	*policewoman [pəˈliːsˌwʊmən]	Polizistin
	* safety ['seɪftɪ]	Sicherheit
	* important [ɪmˈpɔːtnt]	wichtig
	* traffic sign ['træfɪk ˌsaɪn]	Verkehrszeichen
	* sign [saɪn]	Zeichen, Schild
	* on foot [ɒn ˈfʊt]	zu Fuß
	* motorist ['məʊtərɪst]	Autofahrer/in
	* get off [ˌget ˈɒf]	absteigen
	* cyclist [ˌsaɪklɪst]	Radfahrer/in
C5	traffic sign ['træfɪk ˌsaɪn]	Verkehrszeichen
	sign [saɪn]	Zeichen, Schild
C6	pump [pʌmp]	Pumpe
	gear ['gɪə]	Gang
	bell [bel]	Klingel, Glocke
	brake [breɪk]	Bremse
	tyre ['taɪə]	Reifen
	chain [tʃeɪn]	Kette
	pedal ['pedl]	Pedal
	well-oiled [wel'ɔɪld]	gut geölt
	clean [kliːn]	sauber
C7	**shout (at)** [ʃaʊt (ət)]	(an)schreien
	us [ʌs]	uns
	track [træk]	Spur, Weg
	biker ['baɪkə]	Radfahrer/in

A hole is a safe place for a mouse.

a sign

clean

Wortfeld

Clothes		
blazer	scarf	tie
boot	shoe	to dress
colour	size	to put on
glove	skirt	to wear
hat	sock	uniform
jacket	sports gear	vest
raincoat	T-Shirt	...

A1	**middle** [mɪdl]	Mitte
A2	**reporter** [rɪˈpɔːtə]	Reporter/in
	ranger [ˈreɪndʒə]	Ranger, Aufseher/in
	alive [əˈlaɪv]	lebendig, am Leben
	cub [kʌb]	Junges *(bei Bären)*
	listener [ˈlɪsnə]	Zuhörer/in
	report [rɪˈpɔːt]	berichten
	rope [rəʊp]	Seil
	down [daʊn]	unten, hinunter
	microphone [ˈmaɪkrəfəʊn]	Mikrofon
	exclusive [ɪkˈskluːsɪv]	Exklusiv-
	hear [hɪə]	hören
	pull [pʊl]	ziehen
	get out of [ˌget_ˈaʊt_əv]	herauskommen, heraus-holen
	ever [ˈevə]	jemals
	fall [fɔːl]	fallen, stürzen
	for (2 hours) [fɔː (ˌtuː ˈaʊəz)]	seit (2 Stunden)
	I'd (= I would) love to [ˌaɪd ˈlʌv tʊ]	ich würde sehr gern
	nothing [ˈnʌθɪŋ]	nichts
	catch a cold [ˌkætʃ_ə ˈkəʊld]	sich erkälten
	worry [ˈwʌrɪ]	sich Sorgen machen
	at the bottom [ət ðə ˈbɒtəm]	unten
	climb [klaɪm]	(hinauf)klettern
A3	helicopter [ˈhelɪkɒptə]	Hubschrauber
	up [ʌp]	oben, hoch, hinauf
A4	*attack [əˈtæk]	angreifen
	*danger [ˈdeɪndʒə]	Gefahr
B1	**dinosaur** [ˈdaɪnəsɔː]	Dinosaurier
	unfriendly [ʌnˈfrendlɪ]	unfreundlich
	tail [teɪl]	Schwanz
	ear [ɪə]	Ohr
	fight [faɪt]	kämpfen
	roar [rɔː]	brüllen
B2	**would** [wʊd]	würde
	museum [mjuːˈzɪəm]	Museum
	something [ˈsʌmθɪŋ]	etwas
	piano [pɪˈænəʊ]	Piano, Klavier
B4	**table tennis** [ˈteɪbl ˌtenɪs]	Tischtennis
B6	supersaurus [ˌsuːpəˈsɔːrəs]	Supersaurier
	* skeleton [ˈskelɪtn]	Skelett
	* suddenly [ˈsʌdnlɪ]	plötzlich
	* crack [kræk]	Krachen
	* rest [rest]	Rest
	* get [get]	*hier:* werden
	* guide [gaɪd]	Führer/in
	* cool down [ˌkuːl ˈdaʊn]	sich beruhigen
C1	**tent** [tent]	Zelt
C2	**rain** [reɪn]	regnen
	concert [ˈkɒnsət]	Konzert

I'd love to fly in a balloon.

friendly ≠ unfriendly

something ≠ nothing

WORDS

Lerntipps

VOKABEL-DOMINO
Für das Vokabel-Domino brauchst du eine/n Partner/in. Du beginnst das Spiel, indem du eine englische Vokabel waagerecht auf ein leeres Blatt Papier schreibst. Nun muss dein/e Partner/in die deutsche Bedeutung deines Wortes nennen. Bei einer richtigen Antwort gibt es einen Punkt und er/sie ist an der Reihe, ein englisches Wort (waagerecht/senkrecht) „anzulegen".
Kennt ihr weitere Spiele, mit denen ihr Vokabeln üben könnt? Probiert doch mal ein selbst gebasteltes Memory. Viel Spaß!

BUNTE BILDER
Um dir Hauptwörter besser zu merken, kannst du Bilder aus Zeitschriften oder Katalogen ausschneiden, z.B. Tiere, Kleider, Lebensmittel. Klebe die Bilder auf ein Blatt in deinen Vokabelordner und schreibe die dazugehörigen Vokabeln direkt an das Bild. So kannst du englische Begriffe richtig „sehen".

WORTFELDER ERGÄNZEN
Wie viele Wortfelder hast du inzwischen in deinem Ordner? Wer hat die meisten? Hier noch eine Liste mit Vorschlägen:

People	Hobbies / free time
Body	Clothes
Food and drink	Time and date
Feelings	Transport
Family	Nature
Pets and animals	Home
School	City / places
Sports	Work / jobs

Wortfeld

Feelings

+	–
happy	alone
friendly	unfriendly
lucky	worried
	frightened
	hungry
like	hate
love	
enjoy	
dream ...	
favourite ...	
Super!	
Well done!	Sorry.
Great/Good idea!	Oh dear!
Thank goodness!	What a pity.
good, better	bad, worse
wonderful	terrible
interesting	boring
exciting	
soft	hard
nice	silly
lovely	
cuddly	
pretty	
beautiful	
peaceful	loud

A

a (year) [ə ('jɪə)] pro (Jahr) II/4B5

a little [ə 'lɪtl] ein bisschen, ein wenig II/3B5

a/an [ə/ən] ein(e) I/1A1

about [ə'baʊt] über, von I/3C2; ungefähr II/2C1

act [ækt] spielen, darstellen II/3C3

* **add** [æd] hinzufügen II/4A3

address [ə'drɛs] Adresse II/4C1

adjective ['ædʒɪktɪv] Adjektiv, Beiwort II/4C4

* **adopt** [ə'dɒpt] adoptieren II/2B5

adventure [əd'vɛntʃə] Abenteuer II/2C1

* **African** ['æfrɪkən] afrikanisch II/2B5

after ['ɑːftə] nach II/1l

afternoon [ɑːftə'nuːn] Nachmittag I/4B3

afterwards ['ɑːftəwədz] danach II/2C4

again [ə'gɛn] noch einmal, wieder I/1C1

against [ə'gɛnst] gegen I/3A1

(2 minutes) ago [(tʊ ˌmɪnɪts) ə'gəʊ] vor (2 Minuten) II/3A4

* **air** [eə] Luft II/3C5

alarm clock [ə'lɑːm ˌklɒk] Wecker II/5B3

alive [ə'laɪv] lebendig, am Leben II/6A2

all [ɔːl] alle(s), ganz I/3A6

all over the world [ɔːl ˌəʊvə ðə 'wɜːld] auf der ganzen Welt II/4A1

alone [ə'ləʊn] allein II/2A2

already [ɔːl'rɛdɪ] schon, bereits I/2B2

also ['ɔːlsəʊ] auch II/2C1

always ['ɔːlweɪz] immer I/4A2

(8) am [(eɪt) ˌeɪ 'ɛm] (8 Uhr) morgens, vormittags II/2C1

and [ænd, ənd] und I/1A1

animal ['ænɪml] Tier I/3C1

another [ə'nʌðə] andere(r, s) I/4C1

answer ['ɑːnsə] Antwort II/1B6

answer ['ɑːnsə] (be)antworten II/3B3

any ['ɛnɪ] irgendwelche, irgendein(e) II/3C2

apartment [ə'pɑːtmənt] Wohnung II/1A4

apple ['æpl] Apfel I/1B2

April ['eɪprl] April I/5B1

aquarium [ə'kweərɪəm] Aquarium II/2A5

arm [ɑːm] Arm I/2A3

around [ə'raʊnd] um ... herum II/1A4

arrow ['ærəʊ] Pfeil II/3A1

art [ɑːt] Kunst II/3B4

as [æz, əz] wie (Vergleich) II/1C1

as [æz, əz] als II/4B5

as ... as [əz ... əz] so ... wie II/4B3

Asian ['eɪʃn] asiatisch, Asiate/Asiatin II/4A3

ask [ɑːsk] fragen I/3A3

ask for ['ɑːsk fɔː] bitten um II/3A1

* **asleep** [ə'sliːp] schlafend II/2B4

astronaut ['æstrənɔːt] Astronaut II/3A1

at [æt] an, bei I/1B4; um (... Uhr) I/2B4

not at all [ˌnɒt ˌə'tˌɔːl] überhaupt nicht II/3B5

at first [ət 'fɜːst] zuerst II/1A6

at home [ət 'həʊm] zu Hause, daheim I/2C1

at last [ət 'lɑːst] endlich II/3A4

at the back [ət ðə 'bæk] hinten II/1C3

at the bottom [ət ðə 'bɒtəm] unten II/6A2

at the front [ət ðə 'frʌnt] vorn II/1C3

at the top [ət ðə 'tɒp] oben II/1C1

* **attack** [ə'tæk] angreifen II/6A4

August ['ɔːgəst] August I/5B1

aunt [ɑːnt] Tante I/5C1

* **awake** [ə'weɪk] wach II/2B4

away [ə'weɪ] weg, fort II/2B1

B

babysit ['beɪbɪsɪt] babysitten II/3C4

back [bæk] zurück I/3C1

at the back [ət ðə 'bæk] hinten II/1C3

* **back-to-back** [ˌbæk tə 'bæk] mit der Rückseite zueinander II/3C5

bad [bæd] schlecht, schlimm II/1B6

bag [bæg] Tasche, Beutel II/4C1

bake [beɪk] backen II/4B4

* **ball** [bɔːl] Kugel II/4A3

balloon [bə'luːn] Ballon I/5A2

ballpoint ['bɔːlpɔɪnt] Kugelschreiber I/1C1

banana [bə'nɑːnə] Banane I/5B3

* **bark** [bɑːk] bellen II/2B4

bath [bɑːθ] Bad II/2B3

bathroom ['bɑːθrʊm] Bad(ezimmer) I/2A1

beach [biːtʃ] Strand II/1A4

bear [beə] Bär II/2C1

beautiful ['bjuːtəfʊl] schön II/2B1

because [bɪ'kɒz] weil II/2B3

bed [bɛd] Bett I/3C7

before [bɪ'fɔː] bevor I/5A7

beginning [bɪ'gɪnɪŋ] Anfang II/4A3

behind [bɪ'haɪnd] hinter I/2A1

bell [bɛl] Klingel, Glocke II/5C6

belong [bɪ'lɒŋ] gehören II/1A2

better ['bɛtə] besser II/4B2

between [bɪ'twiːn] zwischen I/6C1

big [bɪg] groß, kräftig I/2A5

bike [baɪk] Fahrrad I/1B2

biker ['baɪkə] Radfahrer/in II/5C7

bird [bɜːd] Vogel I/3C3

birthday ['bɜːθdeɪ] Geburtstag I/5B1

Happy birthday! [ˌhæpɪ 'bɜːθdeɪ] Alles Gute zum Geburtstag! I/5B2

* **bite** [baɪt] beißen II/2B4

black [blæk] schwarz I/1B3

* **blind** [blaɪnd] Blinde/r II/2B4

* **blow (up)** [ˌbləʊ ˌ('ʌp)] (auf)blasen II/3C5

blue [bluː] blau I/1B3

board [bɔːd] Tafel I/1C2

boat [bəʊt] Boot II/1A4

body ['bɒdɪ] Körper I/2l

bone [bəʊn] Knochen II/1A4

book [bʊk] Buch I/1B2

boot [buːt] Stiefel II/3B1

boring ['bɔːrɪŋ] langweilig I/4C7

* **born** [bɔːn] geboren II/2B5

both [bəʊθ] beide II/1B2

bottle ['bɒtl] Flasche II/4A5

at the bottom [ət ðə 'bɒtəm] unten II/6A2

bow [bəʊ] Bogen II/3A1
* bowl [bəʊl] Schüssel II/4A3
box [bɒks] Schachtel, Kiste I/3C3
boy [bɔɪ] Junge I/1A7
brake [breɪk] Bremse II/5C6
bread [bred] Brot I/2C1
break [breɪk] Pause I/5A5
break [breɪk] brechen II/5C2
* break of day [ˌbreɪk əv ˈdeɪ] Tagesanbruch II/3C6
breakfast [ˈbrekfəst] Frühstück I/2B1
bridge [brɪdʒ] Brücke II/2C1
brilliant [ˈbrɪljənt] brillant, großartig II/4B1
bring [brɪŋ] (mit)bringen I/3A1
British [ˈbrɪtɪʃ] britisch I/6A1
brochure [ˈbrəʊʃə] Broschüre II/2C5
brother [ˈbrʌðə] Bruder I/2C4
brown [braʊn] braun I/1B2
bubble [ˈbʌbl] Blase II/5A6
building [ˈbɪldɪŋ] Gebäude II/1A4
Bunsen burner [ˌbʌnsn ˈbɜːnə] Bunsenbrenner II/1C2
bus [bʌs] Bus II/2C2
busker [ˈbʌskə] Straßenmusikant/in II/3C2
busy [ˈbɪzɪ] beschäftigt I/4B1
but [bʌt] aber I/1B2
butter [ˈbʌtə] Butter I/2C3
buy [baɪ] kaufen I/4B3
by [baɪ] hier: bis II/5B2
bye [baɪ] Tschüss! I/3A3

C

cage [keɪdʒ] Käfig II/2A1
cake [keɪk] Kuchen, Torte I/5C2
calculator [ˈkælkjəleɪtə] Taschenrechner II/1C2
call [kɔːl] nennen, rufen I/4C1
it's called [ɪts ˈkɔːld] es heißt I/3B4
camera [ˈkæmrə] Kamera, Fotoapparat I/6A4
camp site [ˈkæmp saɪt] Campingplatz II/1B6
can [kæn] Dose II/1A5
can [kæn] können I/1C1
candle [ˈkændl] Kerze II/4A3
cannon [ˈkænən] Kanone II/2C1
cap [kæp] Mütze I/1A1
car [kɑː] Auto I/6A3
card [kɑːd] Karte II/4A2

careful [ˈkeəfʊl] vorsichtig, behutsam II/3A4
caretaker [ˈkeəˌteɪkə] Hausmeister II/1C6
carrot [ˈkærət] Möhre, Karotte I/3C7
carry [ˈkærɪ] tragen, hier: mitnehmen II/5C2
cassette [kəˈset] Kassette I/5B3
castle [ˈkɑːsl] Schloss II/1A4
cat [kæt] Katze I/3C7
catch [kætʃ] fangen II/2A2
catch a cold [ˌkætʃ ə ˈkəʊld] sich erkälten II/6A2
cattle [ˈkætl] Vieh II/3A1
cauliflower [ˈkɒlɪˌflaʊə] Blumenkohl II/4B4
CD (compact disc) [siːˈdiː] CD I/1A1
CD player [siː ˈdiː ˌpleɪə] CD-Spieler I/4A3
celebrate [ˈselɪbreɪt] feiern II/4A3
celebration [ˌselɪˈbreɪʃn] Feier II/4A3
chain [tʃeɪn] Kette II/5C6
chair [tʃeə] Stuhl I/1C2
championship [ˈtʃæmpjənʃɪp] Meisterschaft II/3B5
* **change** [tʃeɪndʒ] (sich) verändern II/3C5
* **chant** [tʃɑːnt] Sprechgesang, Rap II/1C5
* **chase** [tʃeɪs] jagen II/2B4
* **cheap** [tʃiːp] billig II/4B2
cheese [tʃiːz] Käse I/2C1
chemical [ˈkemɪkl] Chemikalie II/4C1
chewing gum [ˈtʃuːɪŋ ˌɡʌm] Kaugummi II/5A6
chicken [ˈtʃɪkɪn] Huhn, Hähnchen I/2C1
child (Mz: children) [tʃaɪld, ˈtʃɪldrn] Kind I/5A2
chimpanzee [ˌtʃɪmpənˈziː] Schimpanse II/2A5
chips [tʃɪps] Pommes frites I/2C1
chocolate [ˈtʃɒklət] Schokolade I/2C1
chocolates (Mz) [ˈtʃɒkləts] Pralinen II/4B1
choose [tʃuːz] (aus)wählen II/2C3
* **chorus** [ˈkɔːrəs] Chor II/3C6
Christmas [ˈkrɪsməs] Weihnachten II/4C4

church [tʃɜːtʃ] Kirche II/4A1
cinema [ˈsɪnəmə] Kino I/4B3
circle [ˈsɜːkl] Kreis II/4C5
city [ˈsɪtɪ] (Groß)Stadt II/4A3
* clap [klæp] klatschen II/3C5
class [klɑːs] Klasse I/1A7
classmate [ˈklɑːsmeɪt] Klassenkamerad/in I/5A2
classroom [ˈklɑːsrʊm] Klassenzimmer I/1C1
clean [kliːn] sauber machen, putzen I/2A7
clean [kliːn] sauber II/5C6
clever [ˈklevə] klug, schlau II/2A1
climb [klaɪm] (hinauf)klettern II/6A2
close [kləʊz] zumachen, schließen II/2A2
* **closed** [kləʊzd] geschlossen II/3C5
clothes [kləʊðz] Kleidung, Kleidungsstücke I/1C8
cloud [klaʊd] Wolke I/5A2
cloudy [ˈklaʊdɪ] wolkig, bewölkt II/1A6
cm (= centimetre) [ˈsentɪˌmiːtə] Zentimeter II/5A6
coffee [ˈkɒfɪ] Kaffee I/2B2
cold [kəʊld] kalt I/2A7
catch a cold [ˌkætʃ ə ˈkəʊld] sich erkälten II/6A2
collect [kəˈlekt] sammeln, abholen I/6A1
colour [ˈkʌlə] Farbe I/1C8
coloured [ˈkʌləd] farbig II/4A3
colourful [ˈkʌləfʊl] farbig, bunt II/5A4
comb [kəʊm] Kamm II/3C2
come [kʌm] kommen I/3A1
Come on! [kʌmˈɒn] Na, komm schon!, Los! I/2A1
come round [ˌkʌm ˈraʊnd] vorbeischauen II/4B5
commentator [ˈkɒmənteɪtə] Berichterstatter II/1B2
compare [kəmˈpeə] vergleichen II/2C5
concert [ˈkɒnsət] Konzert II/6C2
cook [kʊk] kochen II/4B6
do the cooking [ˌduː ðə ˈkʊkɪŋ] kochen I/4A2
* **cool down** [ˌkuːl ˈdaʊn] sich beruhigen II/6B6
correct [kəˈrekt] korrigieren II/4A2

cosmetics *(Mz)* [kɒz'metɪks] Kosmetika II/5A3

could [kʊd] konnte, könnte II/4C2

count [kaʊnt] zählen I/3B3

country ['kʌntrɪ] Land II/1A4

of course [əv 'kɔːs] selbstverständlich I/3A1

cousin ['kʌzn] Cousin/e I/1A1

* **cover** ['kʌvə] bedecken II/3C5

cow [kaʊ] Kuh I/6B3

* **crack** [kræk] Krachen II/6B6

crazy ['kreɪzɪ] verrückt II/3C2

crocodile ['krɒkədaɪl] Krokodil II/2A3

cross [krɒs] überqueren II/1B4

crown [kraʊn] Krone II/4B5

cub [kʌb] Junges *(bei Bären)* II/6A2

cuddly ['kʌdlɪ] kuschlig II/2B3

cup [kʌp] Tasse I/4C3

custom ['kʌstəm] Brauch, Sitte II/4A1

cycle ['saɪkl] Rad fahren II/1B6

cycling ['saɪklɪŋ] Radfahren II/5C1

* **cyclist** [ˌsaɪklɪst] Radfahrer/in II/5C4

D

dad [dæd] Papa I/4A2

dance [dɑːns] Tanz II/4A3

dance [dɑːns] tanzen I/5C2

* **danger** ['deɪndʒə] Gefahr II/6A4

dangerous ['deɪndʒərəs] gefährlich II/2A1

dark [dɑːk] dunkel II/5B2

date [deɪt] Datum I/5B1

daughter ['dɔːtə] Tochter I/5C5

day [deɪ] Tag I/4B3

one day [wʌn 'deɪ] eines Tages II/3C2

dear [dɪə] liebe(r, s) I/5B1

December [dɪ'sembə] Dezember I/5B1

decorate ['dekəreɪt] dekorieren, schmücken II/4A1

decoration [ˌdekə'reɪʃn] Dekoration, Schmuck II/4A2

* **deep** [diːp] tief II/4A3

delicious [dɪ'lɪʃəs] köstlich, lecker II/4A3

department [dɪ'pɑːtmənt] Abteilung II/4B2

department store [dɪ'pɑːtmənt ˌstɔː] Kaufhaus II/4B2

deputy head [ˌdepjʊtɪ 'hed] Konrektor II/5B2

describe [dɪ'skraɪb] beschreiben II/1C6

desk [desk] Schreibtisch I/1C2

dialogue ['daɪəlɒg] Dialog II/4C7

dictionary ['dɪkʃənrɪ] Wörterbuch II/5C1

diet ['daɪət] Diät II/5B2

different ['dɪfrənt] verschieden II/4A3

difficult ['dɪfɪkəlt] schwierig I/3A3

dinner ['dɪnə] Abendessen I/2C2

dinosaur ['daɪnəsɔː] Dinosaurier II/6B1

do [duː] machen, tun I/3B3

do a paper round [ˌduː ə 'peɪpə raʊnd] Zeitungen austragen II/3C4

dog [dɒg] Hund I/1B2

doll [dɒl] Puppe II/2C1

dolphin ['dɒlfɪn] Delfin II/2A6

door [dɔː] Tür I/1C2

dos and dont's [ˌduːz ən 'dɒnts] Gebote und Verbote II/5I

* **dough** [dəʊ] Teig II/4A3

down [daʊn] unten, hinunter II/6A2

draw [drɔː] zeichnen II/2C5

dream [driːm] Traum II/3A2

dream [driːm] träumen II/3A1

dress up [ˌdres 'ʌp] sich verkleiden II/4B5

drink [drɪŋk] Getränk I/1C8

drink [drɪŋk] trinken I/4C7

dry [draɪ] trocken II/1A4

duck [dʌk] Ente I/2A7

dye [daɪ] färben II/5A3

E

ear [ɪə] Ohr II/6B1

early ['ɜːlɪ] früh II/1C4

earn [ɜːn] verdienen II/3C4

earring ['ɪəˌrɪŋ] Ohrring II/5A2

easy ['iːzɪ] leicht, einfach I/4C3

eat [iːt] essen, fressen I/3C1

egg [eg] Ei I/2B2

* **elastic band** [ɪˌlæstɪk 'bænd] Gummiband II/3C5

elephant ['elɪfənt] Elefant II/2A3

empty ['emptɪ] leer II/1A5

end [end] Ende II/1A6

end [end] aufhören, enden II/1C4

ending ['endɪŋ] Endung II/4B3

English ['ɪŋglɪʃ] englische(r, s) I/1C2

enjoy [ɪn'dʒɔɪ] genießen II/1A5

enough [ɪ'nʌf] genug II/1C4

envelope ['envələʊp] (Brief)Umschlag II/1C2

eraser [ɪ'reɪzə] Radiergummi II/1C2

European [ˌjʊərə'piːən] europäisch II/2C1

even ['iːvn] sogar II/2C1

evening ['iːvnɪŋ] Abend I/4B3

ever ['evə] jemals II/6A2

every ['evrɪ] jede(r, s) I/4B3

everyone ['evrɪwʌn] jede/r II/1A4

everything ['evrɪθɪŋ] alles II/1A4

* **everywhere** ['evrɪweə] überall(hin) II/2B4

example [ɪg'zɑːmpl] Beispiel II/1A2

* **for example** [fər ɪg'zɑːmpl] zum Beispiel II/2B5

exciting [ɪk'saɪtɪŋ] aufregend I/3B5

exclusive [ɪk'skluːsɪv] Exklusiv- II/6A2

Excuse me. [ɪk'skjuːz miː] Entschuldigung! I/6B1

exercise book ['eksəsaɪz ˌbʊk] Schulheft I/1C2

expensive [ɪk'spensɪv] teuer II/4B2

eye [aɪ] Auge I/2A1

F

fairy tale ['feərɪ ˌteɪl] Märchen II/3A3

fall [fɔːl] fallen, stürzen II/6A2

false [fɔːls] falsch II/1B4

family ['fæmlɪ] Familie, Verwandtschaft I/3A1

famous ['feɪməs] berühmt II/2C1

fantastic [fæn'tæstɪk] fantastisch I/2B2

farm [fɑːm] Bauernhof I/3C7

fast [fɑːst] schnell I/3A3

* **fat** [fæt] dick, fett II/2B4

father ['fɑːðə] Vater I/1B2

favourite ['feɪvrɪt] Lieblings(ding, -person) I/1C8

February ['februərɪ] Februar I/5B1

feed [fiːd] füttern I/4C3

* **felt tip** [ˌfel'tɪp] Filzstift II/1C5

festival ['festəvl] Feier, Festival II/1A5

a few [ə 'fjuː] ein paar II/3A4

field [fiːld] Feld II/2A5

fight [faɪt] kämpfen II/6B1

* **fill** [fɪl] füllen II/3C5

find [faɪnd] finden I/3A1

find out [ˌfaɪnd_'aʊt] herausfinden II/4A2

fine [faɪn] fein, gut II/3B5

* **finger** ['fɪŋgə] Finger II/3C5

finishing line ['fɪnɪʃɪŋ laɪn] Ziellinie II/1B2

fireworks ['faɪəˌwɜːks] Feuerwerk II/4A1

at first [ət 'fɜːst] zuerst II/1A6

fish [fɪʃ] Fisch(e) I/2A7

flamingo [flə'mɪŋgəʊ] Flamingo II/2B3

* **flat** [flæt] flach, platt II/4A3

flipper ['flɪpə] Flosse II/2B3

* **flour** ['flaʊə] Mehl II/4A3

flower ['flaʊə] Blume I/4B1

fly [flaɪ] fliegen II/2A5

fog [fɒg] Nebel II/1A6

foggy ['fɒgɪ] neblig II/1A6

* **fold** [fəʊld] falten II/3C5

follow ['fɒləʊ] folgen II/3A4

food [fuːd] Essen, Lebensmittel I/1C8

* **on foot** [ɒn 'fʊt] zu Fuß II/5C4

foot (Mz: feet) [fʊt, fiːt] Fuß I/2A1

for [fɔː, fə] für I/1C1

for (2 hours) [fɔː (ˌtuː 'aʊəz)] seit (2 Stunden) II/6A2

* **for example** [fər_ɪg'zaːmpl] zum Beispiel II/2B5

forest ['fɒrɪst] Wald II/3A4

forget [fə'get] vergessen II/1A1

form [fɔːm] Form II/1B5

* **form** [fɔːm] formen, bilden II/4A3

free [friː] umsonst I/6A1

French [frentʃ] Französisch II/5A5

fresh [freʃ] frisch II/4C1

Friday ['fraɪdeɪ] Freitag I/3B2

friend [frend] Freund/in I/1I

friendly ['frendlɪ] freundlich II/1A4

be frightened [bɪ 'fraɪtnd] Angst haben II/2A2

from [frɒm, frəm] von, aus I/1A1

in front [ɪn 'frʌnt] vorn II/1B2

at the front [ət ðə 'frɒnt] vorn II/1C3

in front of [ɪn 'frʌnt_əv] vor I/2A1

fruit [fruːt] Obst, Frucht I/5B3

full [fʊl] voll II/4A5

fun [fʌn] Spaß II/1B2

funny ['fʌnɪ] lustig, komisch II/2B3

fur [fɜː] Fell, Pelz II/2B3

G

game [geɪm] Spiel I/4B3

garden ['gɑːdn] Garten II/2A2

gear ['gɪə] Gang II/5C6

* **gecko** ['gekəʊ] Gecko II/2B5

geography [dʒɪ'ɒgrəfɪ] Erdkunde, Geographie II/5A5

German ['dʒɜːmən] deutsche(r, s) I/1C1

get [get] bekommen I/5B3

* **get** [get] hier: werden II/6B6

* **get late** [ˌget 'leɪt] spät werden II/3C6

* **get off** [ˌget_'ɒf] absteigen II/5C4

get out of [ˌget_'aʊt_əv] herauskommen, herausholen II/6A2

get ready [ˌget 'redɪ] sich fertig machen II/3C2

get to ['get tʊ] hier: hinkommen II/3A4

get up [get_'ʌp] aufstehen I/5A7

* **giant** ['dʒaɪənt] Riesen- II/2B5

* **giraffe** [dʒə'rɑːf] Giraffe II/2A4

girl [gɜːl] Mädchen I/1A1

give [gɪv] geben I/3A1

glass [glɑːs] Glas II/4A5

glasses (Mz) ['glɑːsɪz] Brille II/3A5

glove [glʌv] Handschuh II/3B1

* **glue** [gluː] Klebstoff, Leim II/1C5

go [gəʊ] gehen I/3B4

go for a walk [ˌgəʊ fər_ə 'wɔːk] einen Spaziergang machen II/4A1

Go on! [gəʊ 'ɒn] Los!, Mach(t) weiter! I/3C1

go out [ˌgəʊ 'aʊt] ausgehen II/5A3

go with ['gəʊ wɪð] passen zu II/3A3

god [gɒd] Gott II/4A3

goddess ['gɒdɪs] Göttin II/4A3

goldfish ['gəʊldfɪʃ] Goldfisch II/4B1

good [gʊd] gut I/1A4

be good at [ˌbɪ 'gʊd_ət] gut sein in/bei II/3B3

Good luck. [ˌgʊd 'lʌk] Viel Glück! II/3B5

good-looking [ˌgʊd 'lʊkɪŋ] gut aussehend II/1A4

grandfather ['grænˌfɑːðə] Großvater I/5C1

grandmother ['grænˌmʌðə] Großmutter I/5C1

grass [grɑːs] Gras II/2A3

great [greɪt] großartig I/1C1

green [griːn] grün I/1B3

grey [greɪ] grau II/5B2

grid [grɪd] Tabelle II/3B2

* **ground** [graʊnd] Boden II/2B4

group [gruːp] Gruppe I/5B3

grow up [ˌgrəʊ_'ʌp] erwachsen werden, groß werden II/3A1

guess [ges] Vermutung, Annahme II/4B1

guess [ges] (er)raten II/6A1

guest [gest] Gast I/4C1

* **guide** [gaɪd] Führer/in II/6B6

guided tour [ˌgaɪdɪd 'tʊə] Führung II/2C5

* **guinea pig** ['gɪnɪ pɪg] Meerschweinchen II/2B5

guitar [gɪ'tɑː] Gitarre II/3C2

gym [dʒɪm] Turnhalle II/1C6

H

hair [heə] Haar(e) I/2A1

* **hairy** ['heərɪ] haarig II/2B4

half [hɑːf] halb II/1C4

hamster ['hæmstə] Hamster II/2A3

hand [hænd] Hand I/2A1

handbag ['hændbæg] Handtasche II/4B2

handkerchief ['hæŋkətʃɪf] Taschentuch II/4B1

handlebar ['hændlbɑː] Lenkstange II/5C2

hang [hæŋ] hängen II/3A4

happen ['hæpən] passieren, geschehen II/6A1

happy ['hæpɪ] glücklich I/3C2

Happy birthday! [ˌhæpɪ
ˈbɜːθdeɪ] Alles Gute zum
Geburtstag! I/5B2

Happy New Year! [ˌhæpɪ njuː
ˈjɪə] Frohes neues Jahr!
II/4A1

hard [hɑːd] hart, schwierig
II/1C3

hat [hæt] Hut, Kopfbedeckung
II/3A4

hate [heɪt] hassen II/1C1

have [hæv] haben I/1C1

have a good time [ˌhæv ə gʊd
ˈtaɪm] sich vergnügen
II/1A1

have a vote [ˌhæv ə ˈvəʊt] eine
Abstimmung machen
II/5B5

have to [ˈhæv tə] müssen II/5A2

* **hay** [heɪ] Heu II/2B5

he [hiː] er I/1A6

head [hed] Kopf I/2A3

headline [ˈhedlaɪn] Überschrift,
Titel II/5C1

headteacher [ˌhedˈtiːtʃə] Direktor/in I/5A2

hear [hɪə] hören II/6A2

* **heat** [hiːt] erhitzen II/4A3

heavy [ˈhevɪ] schwer II/5A6

hedge [hedʒ] Hecke II/1B2

helicopter [ˈhelɪkɒptə] Hubschrauber II/6A3

Hello! [həˈləʊ] Hallo! I/1A1

helmet [ˈhelmɪt] Helm II/5C2

help [help] Hilfe II/2A2

help [help] helfen I/2C1

her [hɜː] ihr(e) I/1A1

here [hɪə] hier I/2C1

Here you are! [ˈhɪə juˌɑː] Bitte
sehr! I/1C1

hero (Mz: heroes) [ˈhɪərəʊ
(ˈhɪərəʊz)] Held II/3A1

high street [ˈhaɪ striːt] Haupt-/
Einkaufsstraße II/4I

Hindu [ˈhɪnduː] Hindu II/4A3

hippopotamus (hippo)
[ˌhɪpəˈpɒtəməs (ˈhɪpəʊ)]
Nilpferd II/2B3

his [hɪz] sein(e) I/1B4

history [ˈhɪstrɪ] Geschichte
II/3B3

* **hit** [hɪt] treffen, schlagen
II/3C5

* **hold** [həʊld] halten II/3C5

hold on to [ˌhəʊld ˈɒn tʊ] sich
festhalten an II/5C2

hole [həʊl] Loch II/2A5

holiday [ˈhɒlədeɪ] Ferien, Urlaub
II/1I

at home [ət ˈhəʊm] zu Hause,
daheim I/2C1

* home country [ˌhəʊm ˈkʌntrɪ]
Heimatland II/2B5

homework [ˈhəʊmwɜːk] Hausaufgabe(n) I/1C1

hope [həʊp] hoffen II/3A4

I hope so. [aɪ ˈhəʊp səʊ] Das
hoffe ich. II/3B5

horror story [ˈhɒrə ˌstɔːrɪ] Gruselgeschichte II/3A3

horse [hɔːs] Pferd II/2A3

hot [hɒt] heiß I/2B4

hotel [həʊˈtel] Hotel II/1B6

hour [ˈaʊə] Stunde II/3C2

house [haʊs] Haus I/3C3

how [haʊ] wie I/1C4

How much is ...? [ˌhaʊ
ˈmʌtʃ əz] Wie viel kostet ...?
I/2C6

hungry [ˈhʌŋgrɪ] hungrig
II/1B2

* **hut** [hʌt] Hütte II/2B5

I

I [aɪ] ich I/1A1

I hope so. [aɪ ˈhəʊp səʊ] Das
hoffe ich. II/3B5

I'd (= I would) love to [ˌaɪd ˈlʌv
tʊ] ich würde sehr gern
II/6A2

I'll (= I will) [aɪl] ich werde
II/3A1

ice [aɪs] Eis II/3B1

ice-cream [ˌaɪsˈkriːm] Eis, Eiskrem I/1B2

ice-skating [ˈaɪsˌskeɪtɪŋ] Schlittschuhlaufen II/3B1

idea [aɪˈdɪə] Idee, Einfall I/1A4

if [ɪf] ob II/6B4

imagine [ɪˈmædʒɪn] sich vorstellen II/2A1

* important [ɪmˈpɔːtnt] wichtig
II/5C4

in [ɪn] in I/1A1

in front [ɪn ˈfrʌnt] vorn II/1B2

in front of [ɪn ˈfrʌnt əv] vor
I/2A1

in short [ɪn ˈʃɔːt] in Kurzform
II/6A3

in the middle [ɪn ðə ˈmɪdl] in
der Mitte II/1C3

* index finger [ˈɪndeks ˌfɪŋgə]
Zeigefinger II/3C5

Indian [ˈɪndjən] indisch(e, er,
es), Inder/in II/4A3

information technology
[ˌɪnfəˈmeɪʃn tekˈnɒlədʒɪ]
Informatik II/3B3

inside [ˌɪnˈsaɪd] innen, drinnen
I/5A7

* **instrument** [ˈɪnstrʊmənt] Instrument II/3C5

interested (in) [ˈɪntrəstɪd (ɪn)]
interessiert (an) I/6B1

interesting [ˈɪntrəstɪŋ] interessant I/1B1

surf the internet [ˌsɜːf ðɪ
ˈɪntənet] im Internet surfen
II/3B3

into [ˈɪntə] in, in ... hinein
II/4B5

introduce (to) [ˌɪntrəˈdjuːs (tə)]
vorstellen, bekannt machen
(mit) II/1C6

invitation [ˌɪnvɪˈteɪʃn] Einladung
I/5B1

it [ɪt] er, sie, es (bei Sachen/Tieren) I/1C1

its [ɪts] sein(e), ihr(e) (bei Sachen/Tieren) I/1B2

J

jacket [ˈdʒækɪt] Jacke I/1A1

January [ˈdʒænjʊərɪ] Januar
I/5B1

Japanese [ˌdʒæpəˈniːz] japanisch
II/2C1

jeans [dʒiːnz] Jeans I/1A1

on the job [ɒn ðə ˈdʒɒb] bei der
Arbeit II/4A2

join [dʒɔɪn] (sich) anschließen
I/6A1

juggler [ˈdʒʌglə] Jongleur/in
II/2C1

juice [dʒuːs] Saft I/2C1

July [dʒʊˈlaɪ] Juli I/5B1

jump [dʒʌmp] (über)springen
II/1B2

June [dʒuːn] Juni I/5B1

just [dʒʌst] nur, gerade, einfach
II/1A1

K

keep [kiːp] behalten, halten
II/4C1

keep on [ˈkiːpˌɒn] bleiben auf
II/5C2

keeper [ˈkiːpə] Wärter/in II/2A2

kg (= kilogramme) [ˈkɪləgræm]
Kilogramm II/5A6

kid [kɪd] Kind II/2C1
kill [kɪl] umbringen II/3A5
king [kɪŋ] König II/2C1
kitchen ['kɪtʃɪn] Küche I/2B2
* **knead** [niːd] kneten II/4A3
know [nəʊ] wissen, kennen II/3A4

L

lamp [læmp] Lampe II/4A3
land [lænd] landen II/1A5
large [lɑːdʒ] groß II/2C1
last [lɑːst] letzte(r, s) I/3B5
last [lɑːst] zuletzt II/2B3
at last [ət 'lɑːst] endlich II/3A4
late [leɪt] (zu) spät I/2B2
later ['leɪtə] später II/2B1
latest ['leɪtɪst] neueste(r, s) II/2A2
lay the table [ˌleɪ ðə 'teɪbl] den Tisch decken II/4B5
learn [lɜːn] lernen I/2A7
leave [liːv] verlassen, weggehen I/5A7
* **leave** [liːv] (be)lassen II/4A3
(on the) left [(ɒn ðə) 'left] links I/1B1
left [left] übrig II/3C2
leg [leg] Bein I/2A3
lemonade [ˌleməˈneɪd] (Zitronen)Limonade I/4C7
lesson ['lesn] (Unterrichts)Stunde, Lektion I/5A5
let off [ˌlet 'ɒf] *hier:* abfeuern II/4A1
letter ['letə] Brief II/1C1
letter ['letə] Buchstabe II/4A5
lie [laɪ] liegen II/1A5
light [laɪt] Licht, Lampe II/3B3
light [laɪt] hell- II/2B3
like [laɪk] mögen, gern haben I/2A7
I don't (= do not) like [aɪ 'dəʊnt laɪk] ich mag nicht I/2B4
like [laɪk] (so) wie II/1A4
like this [laɪk 'ðɪs] so II/1A3
What's ... like? [wɒts ... 'laɪk] Wie ist ...?, Wie sieht ... aus? I/4A2
lion ['laɪən] Löwe II/2B3
* lipstick ['lɪpstɪk] Lippenstift II/4C6
listen (to) ['lɪsn (tə)] hören (auf), zuhören I/3A3
listener ['lɪsnə] Zuhörer/in II/6A2

* litre ['liːtə] Liter II/2B5
little [lɪtl] klein II/3A5
a little [ə 'lɪtl] ein bisschen, ein wenig II/3B5
live [lɪv] leben, wohnen II/1A1
living-room ['lɪvɪŋrʊm] Wohnzimmer I/2B2
locomotive ['ləʊkəˈməʊtɪv] Lokomotive II/2C1
Londoner ['lʌndənə] Londoner/in II/2C1
long [lɒŋ] lang I/2A4
look (at) [lʊk (ət)] (an)schauen I/2A4
look after [ˌlʊk 'ɑːftə] sich kümmern um I/1A1
look for ['lʊk fə] suchen nach I/5C1
look like ['lʊk laɪk] aussehen (wie) I/6C5
* **Lord** [lɔːd] Lord II/4C6
lose [luːz] verlieren II/3B5
loser ['luːzə] Verlierer I/3B5
a lot of [ə 'lɒt əv] viel(e), eine Menge I/1B1
loud [laʊd] laut I/6B4
Love [lʌv] Herzliche Grüße *(Briefschluss)* II/1A4
love [lʌv] lieben I/1C1
lovely ['lʌvlɪ] reizend, nett, süß I/3C1
low [ləʊ] niedrig, tief II/5C2
Good luck. [ˌgʊd 'lʌk] Viel Glück! II/3B5
be lucky [bɪ 'lʌkɪ] Glück haben II/2B1
lunch [lʌntʃ] Mittagessen I/2C1

M

m (= metre) ['miːtə] Meter II/5A6
* **M'lord** [mɪˈlɔːd] Mein Herr *(Anrede eines Lords)* II/4C6
madam ['mædəm] gnädige Frau *(Anrede)* II/4C1
magazine [ˌmægəˈziːn] Zeitschrift II/1C2
maid [meɪd] Dienstmädchen II/4B5
make [meɪk] machen, tun I/4A2
malaria mosquito [məˈleərɪə məˌskɪtəʊ] Malariamücke II/5A6
man (Mz: men) [mæn, men] Mann I/1B2
many ['menɪ] viele II/3C2

how many? [ˌhaʊ 'menɪ] wie viele? I/5A6
map [mæp] Stadtplan, Landkarte II/1C2
March [mɑːtʃ] März I/5B1
market ['mɑːkɪt] Markt I/1A1
match [mætʃ] Wettkampf, -spiel I/3A1
match [mætʃ] passend zusammenfügen II/3A3
maths [mæθs] Mathe I/5A2
What's the matter? [ˌwɒts ðə 'mætə] Was ist los? II/2A2
May [meɪ] Mai I/5B1
may [meɪ] dürfen II/4C1
meal [miːl] Mahlzeit II/2A2
mean [miːn] bedeuten, meinen II/2C1
meat [miːt] Fleisch II/2A3
meet [miːt] (sich) treffen, kennen lernen I/4B3
* **mess about** [ˌmes ə'baʊt] herumspielen II/5B2
microphone ['maɪkrəfəʊn] Mikrofon II/6A2
middle [mɪdl] Mitte II/6A1
in the middle [ɪn ðə 'mɪdl] in der Mitte II/1C3
midnight ['mɪdnaɪt] Mitternacht II/2C1
milk [mɪlk] Milch I/2B2
mindmap ['maɪndmæp] Wortnetz II/3C1
minute ['mɪnɪt] Minute I/3B3
Miss [mɪs] Fräulein *(Anrede)* I/2A5
mistake [mɪˈsteɪk] Fehler II/4A2
* **mix** [mɪks] mixen, mischen II/4A3
model [mɒdl] Modell II/2C1
modern ['mɒdən] modern II/2C1
Monday ['mʌndeɪ] Montag I/3B2
money ['mʌnɪ] Geld II/2C2
month [mʌnθ] Monat I/1C1
moon [muːn] Mond II/2C1
more [mɔː] mehr II/2C1
morning ['mɔːnɪŋ] Morgen, Vormittag I/3C7
most [məʊst] die meisten, am meisten II/4A3
mother ['mʌðə] Mutter I/2A7
* **motorist** ['məʊtərɪst] Autofahrer/in II/5C4
mountain ['maʊntɪn] Berg II/5A6

mouse (Mz: mice) [maʊs, maɪs] Maus II/1C2

mouth [maʊθ] Mund, Maul II/2B3

move [muːv] (sich) bewegen II/1C1

Mr ['mɪstə] Herr (Anrede) I/1B2

Mrs ['mɪsɪz] Frau (Anrede) I/2A5

much [mʌtʃ] viel, sehr II/1A4

mum [mʌm] Mama I/2A1

museum [mjuːˈzɪəm] Museum II/6B2

music ['mjuːzɪk] Musik I/5A5

* musical instrument [ˌmjuːzɪkl 'ɪnstrʊmənt] Musikinstrument II/3C5

Muslim ['mʊslɪm] Moslem/ Moslime II/4A3

must [mʌst] müssen I/4A2

mustn't (= must not) ['mʌsnt] nicht dürfen II/5A2

my [maɪ] mein(e) I/1A1

name [neɪm] Name I/1A1

near [nɪə] nahe, in der Nähe (von) II/1A4

* neck [nek] Hals II/2B4

need [niːd] brauchen, benötigen I/6A1

needn't (= need not) ['niːdnt] nicht brauchen, nicht müssen II/4B2

neighbour ['neɪbə] Nachbar/in II/4A1

never ['nevə] niemals I/4B3

new [njuː] neu I/1C1

New Year [ˌnjuː 'jɪə] Neujahr II/4A3

New Year's Eve [ˌnjuː jɪəz 'iːv] Silvester II/4A2

news [njuːz] Nachrichten II/2A2

newspaper ['njuːspeɪpə] Zeitung II/4C1

newsreader ['njuːz̩riːdə] Nachrichtensprecher/in II/2A2

next [nekst] nächste(r, s) I/3B5

next time ['nekst taɪm] das nächste Mal II/3A4

next to ['nekst tə] neben I/2C1

nice [naɪs] schön, nett I/3C1

* night [naɪt] Nacht, Abend II/2B4

no [nəʊ] nein I/1A5

no [nəʊ] kein(e) II/1A6

noise [nɔɪz] Lärm, Geräusch I/6B4

noisy ['nɔɪzɪ] laut I/5B3

nose [nəʊz] Nase II/3A5

not [nɒt] nicht I/2A7

not at all [ˌnɒt̩əˈt̩ɔːl] überhaupt nicht II/3B5

note [nəʊt] Notiz II/5B2

take notes [ˌteɪk 'nəʊts] sich Notizen machen II/1B6

nothing ['nʌθɪŋ] nichts II/6A2

notice ['nəʊtɪs] Notiz II/4C1

noun [naʊn] Substantiv, Hauptwort II/4C4

November [nəʊˈvembə] November I/5B1

now [naʊ] nun, jetzt I/2C1

now that ['naʊ ðət] jetzt da II/6C4

number ['nʌmbə] Zahl, Nummer I/1C4

... o'clock [əˈklɒk] ... Uhr I/2A1

oak [əʊk] Eiche II/3A4

October [ɒkˈtəʊbə] Oktober I/5B1

of [ɒv, əv] von I/1B1

off [ɒf] weg, fort, los II/1B2

Off you go! [ˌɒf jʊ 'gəʊ] Fort mit dir/euch! II/3C2

often ['ɒfn] oft I/4B3

Oh dear (me)! [ˌəʊ 'dɪə (miː)] Ach je!, Du liebe Zeit! II/1B2

old [əʊld] alt I/1C4

on [ɒn] auf I/2B2

on the job [ɒn ðə 'dʒɒb] bei der Arbeit II/4A2

on the left [ɒn ðə 'left] links I/1B1

on the right [ɒn ðə 'raɪt] rechts I/1B1

once [wʌns] einmal, einst II/3A4

one day [wʌn 'deɪ] eines Tages II/3C2

only ['əʊnlɪ] nur I/2A7

* onto ['ɒntuː] auf II/3C5

open ['əʊpən] öffnen II/4C1

open ['əʊpən] offen I/6A4

open day ['əʊpən ˌdeɪ] Tag der offenen Tür II/1C6

open up [ˌəʊpən̩ˈʌp] aufmachen, sich öffnen II/2C1

* opening ['əʊpnɪŋ] Öffnung II/3C5

or [ɔː] oder I/2B4

orange ['ɒrɪndʒ] Orange I/2B4

order ['ɔːdə] Reihenfolge II/6A3

organize ['ɔːgənaɪz] ordnen II/4A4

other ['ʌðə] andere(r, s) II/1A4

our ['aʊə] unser(e) I/1A7

be out [bɪ 'aʊt] unterwegs/draußen sein II/4B2

go out [ˌgəʊ 'aʊt] ausgehen II/5A3

out of ['aʊt̩əv] aus ... heraus II/1A1

outside [ˌaʊt'saɪd] außerhalb, draußen I/6A1

over ['əʊvə] über II/3C2

over there [əʊvə 'ðeə] da drüben, dort I/2C1

Over to you. [ˌəʊvə tʊ 'juː] Weiter mit dir/euch! II/3I

own [əʊn] eigene(r, s) II/4A3

packed lunch [ˌpækt 'lʌntʃ] Lunchpaket II/5B2

page [peɪdʒ] Seite II/4A3

pair ['peə] Paar II/1B5

* pan [pæn] Pfanne II/4A3

* panda ['pændə] Panda II/2B5

paper ['peɪpə] Papier II/3C2

* paper clip ['peɪpə klɪp] Büroklammer II/1C5

do a paper round [ˌduː ə 'peɪpə raʊnd] Zeitungen austragen II/3C4

parents ['peərnts] Eltern I/4C1

park [pɑːk] Park I/1B1

* part [pɑːt] Teil II/4C6

pass [pɑːs] vorbeigehen, hier: durchfahren II/2C1

passenger ['pæsɪndʒə] Beifahrer/in, Mitfahrer/in II/5C2

past [pɑːst] Vergangenheit II/2C1

past [pɑːst] nach II/1C4

peaceful ['piːsfʊl] friedlich II/2A6

pedal ['pedl] Pedal II/5C6

* pedal ['pedl] in die Pedale treten II/5C3

pen [pen] Füllfederhalter, Füller I/1C2

pencil ['pensl] Bleistift I/1C1

* pencil case ['pensl ˌkeɪs] Federmäppchen II/1C5

penfriend ['penfrend] Brieffreund/in II/5A2

people ['piːpl] Leute I/1C8

perfume ['pɜːfjuːm] Parfüm II/4B1

perhaps [pə'hæps] vielleicht I/2C2

person ['pɜːsn] Person II/3A3

personal ['pɜːsnl] persönlich II/5A5

pet [pet] Haustier I/3C5

phone [fəʊn] anrufen II/4C3

phonecard ['fəʊnkɑːd] Telefonkarte I/6A3

photo ['fəʊtəʊ] Foto II/1A1

piano [pɪ'ænəʊ] Piano, Klavier II/6B2

pick up [ˌpɪk_'ʌp] (in die Hand) nehmen II/4C1

picnic ['pɪknɪk] Picknick I/4C1

picture ['pɪktʃə] Bild I/1C2

pig [pɪg] Schwein I/3C7

pilot ['paɪlət] Pilot/in II/3A2

pink [pɪŋk] rosa II/5A2

What a pity. [ˌwɒt_ə 'pɪtɪ] Wie schade! II/4B5

place [pleɪs] Ort, Platz II/1A4

plan [plæn] Plan II/4A3

plan [plæn] planen II/1C6

plane [pleɪn] Flugzeug II/2C1

plant [plɑːnt] Pflanze II/2A3

plastic bag [ˌplæstɪk 'bæg] Plastiktüte I/6B4

play [pleɪ] spielen I/3A3

player ['pleɪə] Spieler/in II/4C5

please [pliːz] bitte I/1C1

(5) pm [ˌpiː 'em] (5 Uhr) nachmittags, abends II/2B3

pocket money ['pɒkɪt ˌmʌnɪ] Taschengeld II/3C2

point [pɔɪnt] Punkt II/3B1

polar bear ['pəʊlə ˌbeə] Eisbär II/2A4

police [pə'liːs] Polizei I/6B4

policeman [pə'liːsmən] Polizist I/6B4

*policewoman [pə'liːsˌwʊmən] Polizistin II/5C4

polite [pə'laɪt] höflich II/4B5

pony ['pəʊnɪ] Pony I/3C6

postcard ['pəʊstkɑːd] Postkarte I/4A2

potato (Mz: potatoes) [pə'teɪtəʊ] Kartoffel I/4C3

present ['preznt] Geschenk I/5B3

present [prɪ'zent] vorstellen II/1C6

presentation [ˌprezn'teɪʃn] Darbietung, Vorführung II/1C6

pretty ['prɪtɪ] hübsch II/4B2

problem ['prɒbləm] Problem II/5A1

programme ['prəʊgræm] Programm I/6C1

prophet ['prɒfɪt] Prophet II/4A3

proud [praʊd] stolz II/3B3

pull [pʊl] ziehen II/6A2

*pull apart [ˌpʊl_ə'pɑːt] auseinander ziehen II/3C5

pullover ['pʊlˌəʊvə] Pullover I/1A1

pump [pʌmp] Pumpe II/5C6

punch [pʌntʃ] Punsch II/4A1

pupil ['pjuːpl] Schüler/in II/1C2

put [pʊt] legen, setzen, stellen I/3C3

put on [ˌpʊt_'ɒn] anziehen II/3A4

Q

quarter (to/past) ['kwɔːtə] Viertel (vor/nach) II/1C4

queen [kwiːn] Königin II/2C1

question ['kwestʃən] Frage I/6B5

quick [kwɪk] schnell I/3C1

quite [kwaɪt] ziemlich II/3B3

R

rabbit ['ræbɪt] Kaninchen I/3C3

race [reɪs] Rennen II/1B1

racecourse ['reɪskɔːs] Rennbahn II/1B2

rain [reɪn] Regen II/1A4

rain [reɪn] regnen II/6C2

raincoat ['reɪnkəʊt] Regenmantel II/4C1

rainy ['reɪnɪ] regnerisch II/2C2

rainy season [ˌreɪnɪ 'siːzn] Regenzeit II/4C1

ranger ['reɪndʒə] Ranger, Aufseher/in II/6A2

*rare [reə] selten, rar II/2B5

*rat [ræt] Ratte II/2B4

read [riːd] lesen II/3A1

ready ['redɪ] fertig, bereit I/2A1

Ready, steady, go! [ˌredɪ ˌstedɪ 'gəʊ] Achtung, fertig, los! II/3B1

real [rɪəl] wirklich, richtig II/4A3

really ['rɪəlɪ] wirklich II/1A1

recipe ['resɪpiː] Rezept II/4A3

record ['rekɔːd] Rekord II/5A6

record [rɪ'kɔːd] aufnehmen II/4C7

red [red] rot I/1A1

reflector [rɪ'flektə] Rückstrahler II/5C2

relax [rɪ'læks] sich entspannen II/2C1

remember [rɪ'membə] (sich) erinnern, denken an II/3A4

repair [rɪ'peə] reparieren II/3C4

repeat [rɪ'piːt] wiederholen II/4C5

report [rɪ'pɔːt] Bericht II/1A5

report [rɪ'pɔːt] berichten II/6A2

reporter [rɪ'pɔːtə] Reporter/in II/6A2

respect [rɪ'spekt] respektieren, achten II/5B2

*rest [rest] Rest II/4A3

*rhythm ['rɪðəm] Rhythmus II/3C5

*rice [raɪs] Reis II/3C5

ride [raɪd] reiten, fahren I/3B3

rider ['raɪdə] Reiter II/1B2

riding lesson ['raɪdɪŋ ˌlesn] Reitstunde II/1B1

right [raɪt] richtig I/1B5

(on the) right [(ɒn ðə) 'raɪt] rechts I/1B1

river ['rɪvə] Fluss II/5A6

road [rəʊd] Straße I/1A1

roar [rɔː] brüllen II/6B1

*roll out [ˌrəʊl_'aʊt] ausrollen II/4A3

room [ruːm] Zimmer, Raum I/3C7

rope [rəʊp] Seil II/6A2

rose [rəʊz] Rose II/4B2

round [raʊnd] rund II/1C3

rucksack ['rʌksæk] Rucksack I/6B1

rule [ruːl] Regel II/5A2

ruler ['ruːlə] Lineal II/1C2

run [rʌn] rennen, laufen I/3A3

S

saddle ['sædl] Sattel II/5C2

safe [seɪf] sicher II/5C1

*safety ['seɪftɪ] Sicherheit II/5C4

salad ['sæləd] Salat I/4A2

*salt [sɔːlt] Salz II/2B5

the same [ðə 'seɪm] der/die/das gleiche II/1C1

Saturday ['sætədeɪ] Samstag I/2B2

sausage ['sɒsɪdʒ] Würstchen I/2B2

say [seɪ] sagen I/1C1

scarf (Mz: scarves) [skɑːf (skɑːvz)] Schal II/3B1

scene [siːn] Szene II/3C3

school [skuːl] Schule I/2B4

school dinner ['skuːl ˌdɪnə] Schulessen II/5B2

school grounds ['skuːl ˌgraʊndz] Schulgelände II/5B2

schoolbag ['skuːlbæg] Schultasche I/1C1

science ['saɪəns] Naturwissenschaft II/1C1

* science lab ['saɪəns ˌlæb] Physiksaal II/5B2

sea [siː] Meer II/1A5

sea lion ['siː ˌlaɪən] Seelöwe II/2A3

seaside ['siːsaɪd] Meeresküste II/1A5

seat [siːt] Sitz II/5C2

second ['sekənd] Sekunde II/3B1

secretary ['sekrətrɪ] Sekretär/in II/1C6

see [siː] sehen I/2A7

See you! ['siː juː] Bis dann! I/3A3

sell [sel] verkaufen I/4B3

semi-final [ˌsemiˈfaɪnl] Halbfinale II/3B5

send [send] senden, schicken II/4A2

sentence ['sentəns] Satz II/1A3

September [sepˈtembə] September I/5B1

serve [sɜːv] servieren II/4B5

several ['sevrəl] mehrere, einige II/2C1

* shake [ʃeɪk] schütteln II/3C5

* shaker ['ʃeɪkə] Shaker, Mixbecher II/3C5

shall [ʃæl] soll II/4B2

* share [ʃeə] teilen II/2B5

shark [ʃɑːk] Hai II/2C1

sharp [ʃɑːp] scharf II/2B3

she [ʃiː] sie I/1A1

* sheep [ʃiːp] Schaf(e) II/2B4

shelf (Mz: shelves) [ʃelf, ʃelvz] Regal I/4A2

ship [ʃɪp] Schiff II/2C1

shirt [ʃɜːt] Hemd II/5B2

* shirtmaker ['ʃɜːtmeɪkə] Hemdenschneider/in II/4C6

shoe [ʃuː] Schuh I/3A5

* shoemaker ['ʃuːmeɪkə] Schuhmacher/in II/4C6

shop [ʃɒp] Geschäft II/2C1

shop window ['ʃɒp wɪndəʊ] Schaufenster II/4B2

shopping ['ʃɒpɪŋ] Einkauf(en) I/2C1

short [ʃɔːt] kurz, klein I/2A5

in short [ɪn 'ʃɔːt] in Kurzform II/6A3

shout (at) [ʃaʊt (ət)] (an)schreien II/5C7

show [ʃəʊ] Vorführung I/6A4

show [ʃəʊ] zeigen I/6A4

shy [ʃaɪ] schüchtern II/3B3

side [saɪd] Seite II/5C2

sight [saɪt] Sehenswürdigkeit II/1A4

sign [saɪn] Zeichen, Schild II/5C5

silly ['sɪlɪ] dumm, blöd II/5A2

simple past [ˌsɪmpl 'pɑːst] einfache Vergangenheit II/4A1

sing [sɪŋ] singen I/3B3

* sir [sɜː] Herr (förmliche Anrede) II/4C6

sister ['sɪstə] Schwester I/2B4

sit [sɪt] sitzen, sich setzen I/5C1

* sit down [ˌsɪt 'daʊn] sich hinsetzen II/3C5

skate [skeɪt] Schlittschuh/Rollschuh/Inlineskates laufen I/3B3

* skeleton ['skelɪtn] Skelett II/6B6

skirt [skɜːt] Rock II/5B2

sky [skaɪ] Himmel I/5A2

sleep [sliːp] schlafen I/4A2

sleepy ['sliːpɪ] schläfrig II/2A1

slim [slɪm] schlank I/2A5

slow [sləʊ] langsam II/2A1

small [smɔːl] klein I/2A6

smell (of) [smel (əv)] riechen, duften, stinken (nach) II/1C1

smoke [sməʊk] Rauch II/1C2

smoke [sməʊk] rauchen II/5B2

snail [sneɪl] Schnecke II/2C1

snake [sneɪk] Schlange II/2A3

snow [snəʊ] Schnee I/4B1

snowman ['snəʊmæn] Schneemann II/3B1

so [səʊ] so I/2A7; also, daher II/1A4

sock [sɒk] Socke, Kniestrumpf I/3A6

soft [sɒft] weich II/1C3

some [sʌm] einige, etwas II/1A5

someone ['sʌmwʌn] jemand II/2A2

something ['sʌmθɪŋ] etwas II/6B2

sometimes ['sʌmtaɪmz] manchmal I/4C3

somewhere ['sʌmweə] irgendwo II/1A5

son [sʌn] Sohn I/5C5

song [sɒŋ] Lied I/5A7

soon [suːn] bald II/1A4

Sorry. ['sɒrɪ] Entschuldigung; Wie bitte? I/1A1; (Es) tut mir Leid! I/1C1

sound [saʊnd] Klang, Geräusch II/4A3

* sound [saʊnd] klingen II/3C5

south [saʊθ] Süden II/1A4

speak [spiːk] sprechen I/3B3

speaker ['spiːkə] Sprecher/in II/2C1

special ['speʃl] besondere(r, s) II/4A2

spend [spend] verbringen II/2C4

spider ['spaɪdə] Spinne II/2C1

* spoon [spuːn] Löffel II/3C5

sports centre ['spɔːts ˌsentə] Sportzentrum I/3B2

sports gear ['spɔːts ˌgɪə] Sportkleidung II/5B2

sportsman ['spɔːtsmən] Sportler II/3A1

sportsperson ['spɔːtsˌpɜːsn] Sportler/in II/2C1

square [skweə] eckig, quadratisch II/1C3

squeeze [skwiːz] drücken II/3B5

stable ['steɪbl] Stall II/1A1

stall [stɔːl] Stand I/5B3

stamp [stæmp] Briefmarke I/6A1

stand [stænd] stehen I/3A5

star [stɑː] Stern II/2C1

start [stɑːt] anfangen, beginnen I/5A5

station ['steɪʃn] Bahnhof, U-Bahn-Station I/4A2

stationery ['steɪʃnərɪ] Schreib-
waren II/4B2

stay [steɪ] bleiben, sich aufhal-
ten II/1A1

stay up late [ˌsteɪ_ʌp 'leɪt] lange
aufbleiben II/5A2

stereo ['sterɪəʊ] Stereoanlage
II/4A3

still [stɪl] noch I/2B2

stone [stəʊn] Stein II/4A5

stop [stɒp] anhalten, aufhören
I/3C1

storm [stɔːm] Sturm I/6A1

story ['stɔːrɪ] Geschichte
I/3C7

strange [streɪndʒ] seltsam,
fremd II/4C1

street [striːt] Straße I/1A1

* **stretch** [stretʃ] dehnen II/3C5

string [strɪŋ] Schnur, Kette
II/4A3

stripe [straɪp] Streifen II/2A1

* **striped** [straɪpt] gestreift II/2B4

strong [strɒŋ] stark II/3A3

subject ['sʌbdʒekt] (Unterrichts)Fach I/5A5

successful [sək'sesfʊl] erfolg-
reich II/5A6

* **suddenly** ['sʌdnlɪ] plötzlich
II/6B6

sugar ['ʃʊgə] Zucker I/2B2

summer ['sʌmə] Sommer
II/1A5

sun [sʌn] Sonne II/1A5

Sunday ['sʌndeɪ] Sonntag
I/3B2

sunflower ['sʌnflaʊə] Sonnen-
blume II/1B4

sunglasses ['sʌnglɑːsɪz] Sonnen-
brille II/4B2

sunny ['sʌnɪ] sonnig II/1A4

supermarket ['suːpəˌmɑːkɪt]
Supermarkt I/1B2

supersaurus [ˌsuːpə'sɔːrəs]
Supersaurier II/6B6

sure [ʃʊə] sicher II/2B1

surf the internet [ˌsɜːf ðɪ
'ɪntənet] im Internet surfen
II/3B3

surprise [sə'praɪz] überraschen
II/6C4

* **surprised** [sə'praɪzd] überrascht
II/4C6

survey ['sɜːveɪ] Umfrage II/6B4

sweets (Mz) [swiːts] Süßigkeiten
II/5A3

swim [swɪm] schwimmen I/2A7

T

table [teɪbl] Tisch I/2B2

lay the table [ˌleɪ ðə 'teɪbl] den
Tisch decken II/4B5

table tennis ['teɪbl ˌtenɪs] Tischtennis II/6B4

* **tablespoon** ['teɪblspuːn] Ess-
löffel II/4A3

tail [teɪl] Schwanz II/6B1

take [teɪk] nehmen, bringen
I/3C1

take for a walk [ˌteɪk fər_ə
'wɔːk] ausführen II/3C4

take notes [ˌteɪk 'nəʊts] sich
Notizen machen II/1B6

talk (to) [tɔːk (tə)] sprechen
(mit) I/4C7

talker ['tɔːkə] Redner/in II/3B5

tall [tɔːl] groß I/2A5

task [tɑːsk] Aufgabe II/4C7

taste [teɪst] Geschmack II/5A5

tea [tiː] Tee I/2B4

teacher ['tiːtʃə] Lehrer/in I/1C1

team [tiːm] Mannschaft I/3A1

* **teaspoon** ['tiːspuːn] Teelöffel
II/4A3

technology [tek'nɒlədʒɪ] Tech-
nik, Technologie II/5A5

telephone ['telɪfəʊn] Telefon
I/1C5

tell [tel] sagen, erzählen I/4B3

tent [tent] Zelt II/6C1

terrible ['terəbl] schrecklich
II/1B6

than [ðæn, ðən] als (bei Vergleichen) II/2A6

Thank goodness! [ˌθæŋk
'gʊdnəs] Gott sei Dank!
II/2A2

thank you ['θæŋk jʊ] danke
I/2B2

thanks [θæŋks] danke I/1A5

that [ðæt] der, die, das (da);
jene(r, s) I/1A1

that [ðæt, ðət] dass II/2B1

the [ðə] der, die, das I/1A1

their [ðeə] ihr(e) (Mz) I/2C1

them [ðem] sie (Mz), ihnen
II/2B1

then [ðen] dann I/3C1

there [ðeə] da(hin), dort(hin)
II/1A1

there are [ðeə'r_ɑː] es gibt, da
sind I/1B1

there is [ðeə'r_ɪz] es gibt, da ist
I/1B3

these [ðiːz] diese (Mz) II/1A1

---

they [ðeɪ] sie (Mz) I/2A7

* **thin** [θɪn] dünn II/2B4

thing [θɪŋ] Ding, Sache I/1B2

think [θɪŋk] denken, glauben,
meinen I/1A1

think about ['θɪŋk_əˌbaʊt] nach-
denken über, denken an
II/1C1

think of ['θɪŋk_əv] sich überle-
gen, denken an II/5A1

this [ðɪs] der, die, das (hier);
diese(r, s) I/1A1

this time ['ðɪs taɪm] dieses Mal
II/3A4

those [ðəʊz] jene, die (da)
II/5A2

through [θruː] durch I/5A2

* **thumb** [θʌm] Daumen II/3C5

Thursday ['θɜːzdeɪ] Donnerstag
I/3B2

tidy ['taɪdɪ] aufräumen I/4C3

tie [taɪ] Krawatte II/5B2

tiger ['taɪgə] Tiger II/2A1

* **tightly** ['taɪtlɪ] fest, eng II/3C5

till [tɪl] bis I/3A3

time [taɪm] Zeit I/2B1

have a good time [ˌhæv_ə gʊd
'taɪm] sich vergnügen
II/1A1

next time ['nekst taɪm] das
nächste Mal II/3A4

this time ['ðɪs taɪm] dieses Mal
II/3A4

Time's up. [ˌtaɪmz_'ʌp] Die Zeit
ist um. II/3B1

What time? [wɒt 'taɪm] Um wie
viel Uhr? II/4A2

What's the time? [ˌwɒts ðə
'taɪm] Wie viel Uhr ist es?
I/2B7

timetable ['taɪmˌteɪbl] Stunden-
plan I/5A5

to [tʊ, tə] zu, nach, für I/3C1;
vor (Uhrzeit) II/2B1

to [tuː, tʊ] hier: bis II/5B2

today [tə'deɪ] heute I/5B3

together [tə'geðə] zusammen
II/1B7

toilet ['tɔɪlɪt] Toilette I/6B1

tomato (Mz: tomatoes)
[tə'mɑːtəʊ (tə'mɑːtəʊz)]
Tomate II/4C1

tomorrow [tə'mɒrəʊ] morgen
I/4B3

ton [tʌn] Tonne II/5A6

tonight [tə'naɪt] heute Abend,
heute Nacht I/4B3

too [tuː] auch I/1A6; (all)zu
I/2A7

*tooth (Mz: teeth) [tuːθ (tiːθ)]
Zahn II/3C5

at the top [ət ðə 'tɒp] oben
II/1C1

topic ['tɒpɪk] Thema II/3B1

tourist ['tʊərɪst] Tourist/in
II/2C1

tower ['tauə] Turm II/2C1

town [taun] Stadt I/3B4

toy [tɔɪ] Spielzeug II/2C1

track [træk] Spur, Weg II/5C7

traffic sign ['træfɪk ˌsaɪn] Ver-
kehrszeichen II/5C5

train [treɪn] Zug, U-Bahn-Wa-
gen I/4B3

tree [triː] Baum I/5A2

trek [trek] Treck, Reise II/3A1

trip [trɪp] Ausflug II/1A4

trousers (Mz) ['trauzəz] Hose(n)
II/5B2

true [truː] wahr I/4C3

*trumpet ['trʌmpɪt] Trompete
II/3C5

trunk [trʌŋk] Rüssel II/2B3

try [traɪ] versuchen II/2A2

tube [tjuːb] U-Bahn (in London)
II/2B1

Tuesday ['tjuːzdeɪ] Dienstag
I/3B2

It's my turn. [ɪts 'maɪ tɜːn] Ich
bin dran. I/4A2

turn [tɜːn] abbiegen, (sich) dre-
hen I/6B2

turn (around) [ˌtɜːn (əˈraund)]
sich (um)drehen II/1B2

tusk [tʌsk] Stoßzahn II/2B3

twice [twaɪs] zweimal II/4A3

type [taɪp] Typ, Art II/3A3

*typical ['tɪpɪkl] typisch II/4C6

tyre ['taɪə] Reifen II/5C6

U

umbrella [ʌmˈbrelə] Regen-
schirm II/4C1

uncle ['ʌŋkl] Onkel I/5C1

under ['ʌndə] unter I/2A7

understand [ʌndəˈstænd] verstehen II/5C1

unfriendly [ʌnˈfrendlɪ] un-
freundlich II/6B1

uniform ['juːnɪfɔːm] Uniform
II/2C1

until [ʌnˈtɪl] bis II/1B7

unusual [ʌnˈjuːʒuəl] ungewöhn-
lich II/4B5

up [ʌp] oben, hoch, hinauf
II/6A3

up and down [ˌʌp_ən 'daun] auf
und ab II/4B2

us [ʌs] uns II/5C7

use [juːz] benutzen, gebrauchen II/1A2

usually ['juːʒuəlɪ] gewöhnlich,
normalerweise II/2A5

V

*vegetable oil ['vedʒtəbl_ɔɪl]
pflanzliches Öl II/4A3

vegetables ['vedʒtəblz] Gemüse
I/2C1

vegetarian [ˌvedʒɪˈteərɪən] Vege-
tarier/in II/5B3

verb [vɜːb] Verb II/1B5

very ['verɪ] sehr I/2A7

vest [vest] Unterhemd II/3B1

vet [vet] Tierarzt, Tierärztin
II/3A2

visit ['vɪzɪt] besuchen II/1A1

visitor ['vɪzɪtə] Besucher/in
II/2C5

have a vote [ˌhæv ə 'vəut] eine
Abstimmung machen
II/5B5

W

wait [weɪt] warten I/3A3

Wait a minute! ['weɪt_ə ˌmɪnɪt]
Moment mal! II/1B2

go for a walk [ˌgəu fər_ə 'wɔːk]
einen Spaziergang machen
II/4A1

take for a walk [ˌteɪk fər_ə
'wɔːk] ausführen II/3C4

walk [wɔːk] (spazieren) gehen
I/4B3

walk up to [ˌwɔːk_'ʌp tə] hin-
gehen zu, sich nähern
II/4C1

want [wɒnt] wollen I/6A1

warm [wɔːm] warm II/1A6

wash [wɒʃ] (sich) waschen
I/2A7

*wash down [ˌwɒʃ 'daun] hinun-
terspülen II/2B5

watch [wɒtʃ] zuschauen, beobachten I/3A1

*Watch out! [ˌwɒtʃ_'aut] Pass
auf! II/5C3

watch TV [ˌwɒtʃ tiː'viː] fernse-
hen I/4B3

water ['wɔːtə] Wasser I/2A7

water ['wɔːtə] gießen II/3C4

wax [wæks] Wachs II/2C1

way [weɪ] Weg II/1A4

we [wiː] wir I/2C4

wear [weə] tragen (Kleidung)
I/3B4

weather ['weðə] Wetter II/1A4

Wednesday ['wenzdeɪ]
Mittwoch I/3B2

week [wiːk] Woche I/4C7

weekend [ˌwiːk'end] Wochen-
ende I/2C1

welcome ['welkəm] willkommen
heißen II/4A3

well [wel] tja, nun, also II/2B1

well [wel] gut II/4B4

Well done! [ˌwel 'dʌn] Gut gemacht! II/1B2

well-oiled [wel'ɔɪld] gut geölt
II/5C6

wet [wet] nass II/1A6

whale [weɪl] Wal II/5A6

what [wɒt] was I/1A1

What a pity. [ˌwɒt_ə 'pɪtɪ] Wie
schade! II/4B5

What about? [wɒt_əˈbaut] Wie
wäre es mit?, Was ist mit?
I/1A4

What is/are ... like? [ˌwɒt_ɪz/ɑː
'laɪk] Wie ist/sind ...? II/4B3

What time? [wɒt 'taɪm] Um wie
viel Uhr? II/4A2

What's the matter? [ˌwɒts ðə
'mætə] Was ist los? II/2A2

wheel [wiːl] Rad II/5C2

when [wen] wann I/3A1; wenn
I/4A2; als II/3B3

where [weə] wo I/1A4

which [wɪtʃ] welche(r, s)
II/1C4

white [waɪt] weiß I/1B3

who [huː] wer I/1A1; der, die,
das (Relativpronomen)
II/5B2

*wholemeal ['həulmiːl] Vollkorn-
II/4A3

why [waɪ] warum II/1C1

wild [waɪld] wild II/2A1

will [wɪl] werden (Zukunft)
II/3A1

win [wɪn] gewinnen I/3B5

wind [wɪnd] Wind I/6B4

window ['wɪndəu] Fenster
II/4A3

windy ['wɪndɪ] windig II/1A6

winner ['wɪnə] Gewinner I/3B5

winter ['wɪntə] Winter I/4I

wish [wɪʃ] Wunsch II/4A1

wish [wɪʃ] wünschen II/1C1
with [wɪð] mit I/2A5
wolf (Mz: wolves) [wʊlf (wʊlvz)] Wolf II/3A5
woman (Mz: women) ['wʊmən, 'wɪmɪn] Frau I/2A5
won't (= will not) [wəʊnt] nicht werden *(Zukunft)* II/3B5
wonderful ['wʌndəfʊl] wunderbar II/4B5
woolly ['wʊlɪ] wollig II/3B1
word [wɜːd] Wort I/1C1
work [wɜːk] Arbeit I/2B2
work [wɜːk] arbeiten I/4B3; funktionieren II/5B3

world [wɜːld] Welt II/2C1
worried ['wʌrɪd] besorgt, beunruhigt II/3B5
worry ['wʌrɪ] sich Sorgen machen II/6A2
worse [wɜːs] schlechter, schlimmer II/5B5
would [wʊd] würde II/6B2
write [raɪt] schreiben I/4C7
write down [ˌraɪt 'daʊn] aufschreiben II/2B2
writing paper ['raɪtɪŋ peɪpə] Briefpapier II/4B1
wrong [rɒŋ] falsch I/1B5

Y

year [jɪə] Jahr I/3B5
year 8 [ˌjɪə'r_eɪt] 6. Klasse II/3B3
yellow ['jeləʊ] gelb I/1B3
yes [jes] ja I/1A4
yesterday ['jestədeɪ] gestern II/1A4
you [juː] du, Sie, ihr I/1A4
young [jʌŋ] jung I/6C1
your [jɔː] dein(e), Ihr(e), euer I/1A1

Z

zoo [zuː] Zoo II/2A1

A

abbiegen, (sich) drehen	turn
Abend	evening
Abendessen	dinner
Abenteuer	adventure
aber	but
abholen	collect
Adresse	address
alle(s), ganz	all
allein	alone
alles	everything
Alles Gute zum Ge burtstag!	Happy birthday!
als	when, as, than (Vergleich)
also, daher	so
alt	old
an	at
andere(r, s)	other, another
Anfang	beginning
anfangen	start
Angst haben	be frightened
anhalten	stop
anrufen	phone
(sich) anschließen	join
(be)antworten	answer
anziehen (Kleidung)	put on
Apfel	apple
April	April
Arbeit	work
arbeiten	work
Arm	arm
auch	too, also
auf	on
aufhören	stop
aufräumen	tidy
aufregend	exciting
aufstehen	get up
Auge	eye
August	August
aus	from
aus ... heraus	out of
ausführen	take for a walk
ausgehen	go out
aussehen (wie)	look like
Auto	car
außerhalb	outside

B

babysitten	babysit
backen	bake
Bad(ezimmer)	bathroom
Bahnhof	station
Ballon	balloon
Banane	banana
Bär	bear
Bauernhof	farm
Baum	tree
bedeuten	mean
beginnen	start
behalten, halten	keep
bei	at
beide	both
Bein	leg
bekommen	get
benötigen	need
beobachten	watch
bereit	ready
bereits	already
berichten	report
berühmt	famous
beschäftigt	busy
besondere(r, s)	special
besorgt, beunruhigt	worried
besser	better
besuchen	visit
Besucher/in	visitor
Bett	bed
Beutel	bag
bevor	before
Bild	picture
billig	cheap
bis	till
Bis dann!	See you!
bitte	please
Bitte sehr!	Here you are!
bitten um	ask for
blau	blue
bleiben, sich auf- halten	stay
Bleistift	pencil
Blume	flower
Blumenkohl	cauliflower
Boot	boat
brauchen	need
braun	brown
Bremse	brake
Brief	letter
Brieffreund/in	penfriend
Briefmarke	stamp
Briefpapier	writing paper
brillant, großartig	brilliant
Brille	glasses (Mz)
(mit)bringen	bring
britisch	British
Brot	bread
Brücke	bridge
Bruder	brother
Buch	book
Bus	bus
Butter	butter

C

CD	CD (compact disc)
CD-Spieler	CD player
Cousin/e	cousin

D

da drüben	over there
da(hin)	there
danach	afterwards
danke	thanks, thank you
dann	then
das	the
das (da)	that
das (hier)	this
das (Relativpronomen)	who
dass	that
Datum	date
dein(e)	your
denken, glauben, meinen	think
der	the
der (da)	that
der (hier)	this
der (Relativpronomen)	who
deutsche(r, s)	German
Dezember	December
die	the
die (da)	that
die (da) (Mz)	those
die (hier)	this
die (Relativpronomen)	who
Dienstag	Tuesday
diese (Mz)	these
diese(r, s)	this
dieses Mal	this time
Ding, Sache	thing
Dinosaurier	dinosaur
Direktor/in	headteacher
Donnerstag	Thursday
dort	over there
dort(hin)	there
draußen	outside
draußen sein	be out
du	you
dumm, blöd	silly
dunkel	dark
durch	through
nicht dürfen	mustn't (= must not)

E

Ei	egg
eigene(r, s)	own
ein bisschen	a little
ein paar	a few
ein wenig	a little
ein(e)	a/an
einige, etwas	some
Einkauf(en)	shopping
Einladung	invitation
einmal, einst	once
Eis	ice
Eis, Eiskrem	ice-cream
Elefant	elephant
Eltern	parents
Ende	end
endlich	at last
englische(r, s)	English
Ente	duck
Entschuldigung	Excuse me, sorry
er	he
er (bei Sachen/Tieren)	it
(sich) erinnern, denken an	remember
Erdkunde	geography
erzählen	tell
es (bei Sachen/Tieren)	it
Essen	food
essen	eat
etwas	something
euer	your

F

(Unterrichts)Fach	subject
fahren	ride
Fahrrad	bike
fallen	fall
falsch	wrong
Familie	family
fangen	catch
fantastisch	fantastic
Farbe	colour
Februar	February
feiern	celebrate
fein, gut	fine
Fenster	window
Ferien	holiday
fernsehen	watch TV
fertig	ready
sich fertig machen	get ready
finden	find
Fisch(e)	fish
Flasche	bottle
Fleisch	meat
fliegen	fly
Flugzeug	plane
Foto	photo
Fotoapparat	camera
Frage	question
fragen	ask
Französisch	French
Frau	woman (Mz: women)
Frau (Anrede)	Mrs
Fräulein (Anrede)	Miss
Freitag	Friday

German	English
fressen	eat
Freund/in	friend
freundlich	friendly
Frucht	fruit
früh	early
Frühstück	breakfast
Füller	pen
Füllfederhalter	pen
funktionieren	work
für	for
füttern	feed
Fuß	foot (Mz: feet)

G

German	English
Gast	guest
geben	give
Geburtstag	birthday
Alles Gute zum Geburtstag!	Happy birthday!
gefährlich	dangerous
gegen	against
gehen	go
(spazieren) gehen	walk
gelb	yellow
Geld	money
Gemüse	vegetables
genießen	enjoy
genug	enough
Geräusch	noise
gern haben	like
Geschäft	shop
Geschenk	present
Geschichte	story, history
gestern	yesterday
Getränk	drink
gewinnen	win
Gewinner	winner
gewöhnlich, normalerweise	usually
Gitarre	guitar
Glas	glass
glauben, meinen, denken	think
Glocke	bell
Viel Glück!	Good luck.
glücklich	happy
Goldfisch	goldfish
Gras	grass
grau	grey
groß	tall, big, large
großartig	great
Großmutter	grandmother
Großvater	grandfather
grün	green
Gruppe	group
gut	good
gut sein in/bei	be good at

German	English
Alles Gute zum Geburtstag!	Happy birthday!

H

German	English
Haar(e)	hair
haben	have
Hähnchen	chicken
halb	half
Hallo!	Hello!
Hamster	hamster
Hand	hand
Handschuh	glove
Handtasche	handbag
hart	hard
hassen	hate
Haus	house
Hausaufgabe(n)	homework
Haustier	pet
heiß	hot
es heißt	it's called
helfen	help
hell-	light
Helm	helmet
Hemd	shirt
Herr *(Anrede)*	Mr
heute	today
heute Abend, heute Nacht	tonight
hier	here
Hilfe	help
Himmel	sky
hinauf	up
hinter	behind
hinunter	down
hoch	up
hoffen	hope
Das hoffe ich.	I hope so.
hören	hear
hören (auf), zuhören	listen (to)
Hose(n)	trousers *(Mz)*
Hotel	hotel
hübsch	pretty
Huhn	chicken
Hund	dog
hungrig	hungry
Hut, Kopfbedeckung	hat

I

German	English
ich	I
Ich bin dran.	It's my turn.
ich würde sehr gern	I'd (= I would) love to
Idee, Einfall	idea
ihnen	them
ihr	you
ihr(e)	her
ihr(e) *(bei Sachen/Tieren)*	its

ihr(e) *(Mz)*	their
Ihr(e)	your
immer	always
in	in
in der Mitte	in the middle
in der Nähe (von)	near
in, in ... hinein	into
Inlineskates laufen	skate
innen, drinnen	inside
interessant	interesting
interessiert (an)	interested (in)
irgendwelche, irgend-ein(e)	any

J

ja	yes
Jacke	jacket
Jahr	year
Januar	January
Jeans	jeans
jede(r, s)	every
jede/r	everyone
jene(r, s)	that
jene (da) *(Mz)*	those
Juli	July
jung	young
Junge	boy
Juni	June

K

Kaffee	coffee
Käfig	cage
kalt	cold
Kamera	camera
kämpfen	fight
Kaninchen	rabbit
Karotte	carrot
Karte	card
Kartoffel	potato (Mz: potatoes)
Käse	cheese
Kassette	cassette
Katze	cat
kaufen	buy
Kaufhaus	department store
Kaugummi	chewing gum
kein(e)	no
kennen	know
Kerze	candle
Kind	child (Mz: children)
Kino	cinema
Klasse	class
6. Klasse	year 8
Klassenkamerad/in	classmate
Klassenzimmer	classroom
Kleidung, Kleidungs-stücke	clothes
klein	short, small, little

(hinauf)klettern	climb
Klingel	bell
klug, schlau	clever
Kniestrumpf	sock
kochen	cook, do the cooking
kommen	come
können	can
konnte, könnte	could
Kopf	head
Körper	body
kräftig	big
Küche	kitchen
Kuchen	cake
Kugelschreiber	ballpoint
Kuh	cow
kurz	short

L

Lampe	light, lamp
Land	country
lang	long
langsam	slow
langweilig	boring
Lärm	noise
laufen	run
laut	noisy, loud
leben	live
Lebensmittel	food
leer	empty
legen	put
Lehrer/in	teacher
leicht, einfach	easy
(Es) tut mir Leid!, Ent-schuldigung!	Sorry.
Lektion	lesson
lernen	learn
lesen	read
letzte(r, s)	last
Leute	people
Licht	light
liebe(r, s)	dear
lieben	love
Lieblings(ding, -per-son)	favourite
Lied	song
(Zitronen)Limonade	lemonade
Lineal	ruler
links	on the left, left
Los!	Go on!, Come on!
lustig, komisch	funny

M

machen, tun	do, make
Mach(t) weiter!	Go on!
Mädchen	girl
Mahlzeit	meal
Mai	May

dieses Mal	this time
das nächste Mal	next time
Mama	mum
manchmal	sometimes
Mann	man (Mz: men)
Mannschaft	team
Markt	market
März	March
Mathe	maths
Maus	mouse (Mz: mice)
Meer	sea
mehr	more
mein(e)	my
meinen	mean
meinen, denken, glauben	think
die meisten, am meisten	most
eine Menge	a lot of
Milch	milk
Minute	minute
mit	with
Mittagessen	lunch
Mitte	middle
in der Mitte	in the middle
Mittwoch	Wednesday
Modell	model
mögen	like
ich mag nicht	I don't (= do not) like
Möhre	carrot
Monat	month
Montag	Monday
Morgen	morning
morgen	tomorrow
(8 Uhr) morgens, vor-mittags	(8) am
Mund, Maul	mouth
Museum	museum
Musik	music
müssen	must, have to
Mutter	mother
Mütze	cap

N

nach	after, past
Nachmittag	afternoon
(5 Uhr) nachmittags, abends	(5) pm
nächste(r, s)	next
das nächste Mal	next time
nahe	near
Name	name
Nase	nose
nass	wet
neben	next to
nehmen, bringen	take
nein	no

nennen, rufen	call
nett	lovely, nice
neu	new
Neujahr	New Year
nicht	not
nichts	nothing
niedrig, tief	low
niemals	never
noch	still
noch einmal	again
November	November
Nummer	number
nun, jetzt	now
nur	only
nur, gerade, einfach	just

O

oben	up
Obst	fruit
oder	or
offen	open
öffnen	open
oft	often
Ohr	ear
Ohrring	earring
Oktober	October
Onkel	uncle
Orange	orange
Ort	place

P

Papa	dad
Papier	paper
Park	park
Pause	break
Person	person
Pferd	horse
Pflanze	plant
Picknick	picnic
Plan	plan
Plastiktüte	plastic bag
Platz	place
Polizei	police
Polizist	policeman
Pommes frites	chips
Pony	pony
Postkarte	postcard
Problem	problem
Programm	programme
Pullover	pullover
Punkt	point
putzen	clean

R

Rad	wheel
Radiergummi	eraser
Raum	room

rechts	on the right, right
Regal	shelf (Mz: shelves)
Regel	rule
Regen	rain
Regenmantel	raincoat
Regenschirm	umbrella
regnen	rain
Reifen	tyre
reiten	ride
reizend	lovely
Rennen	race
rennen	run
reparieren	repair
Reporter/in	reporter
richtig	right
Rock	skirt
Rollschuh laufen	skate
rosa	pink
rot	red
Rucksack	rucksack
rund	round

S

Saft	juice
sagen	say, tell
Salat	salad
sammeln	collect
Samstag	Saturday
Sattel	saddle
sauber	clean
sauber machen	clean
Schachtel, Kiste	box
Schal	scarf (Mz: scarves)
(an)schauen	look (at)
schicken	send
Schiff	ship
Schild	sign
schlafen	sleep
schlank	slim
schlecht, schlimm	bad
schließen	close
Schlittschuh laufen	skate
Schlittschuhlaufen	ice-skating
Schnee	snow
Schneemann	snowman
schnell	fast, quick
Schokolade	chocolate
schon	already
schön	nice, beautiful
schrecklich	terrible
schreiben	write
Schreibtisch	desk
(an)schreien	shout (at)
Schuh	shoe
Schule	school
Schüler/in	pupil
Schulheft	exercise book

Schultasche	schoolbag
schwarz	black
Schwein	pig
schwer	heavy
Schwester	sister
schwierig	difficult, hard
schwimmen	swim
sehen	see
sehr	very, much
sein(e)	his
sein(e) (bei Sachen/ Tieren)	its
Seite	page (Buch), side of course
selbstverständlich	
senden	send
September	September
setzen	put
sich setzen	sit
sicher	sure (gewiss), safe (geschützt)
sie	she
sie (bei Sachen/Tieren)	it
sie (Mz)	they
sie (Akkusativ, Mz)	them
Sie	you
Silvester	New Year's Eve
singen	sing
sitzen	sit
so	so
so ... wie	as ... as
Socke	sock
Sohn	son
Sommer	summer
Sonne	sun
Sonnenbrille	sunglasses
sonnig	sunny
Sonntag	Sunday
sich Sorgen machen	worry
(zu) spät	late
später	later
einen Spaziergang machen	go for a walk
Spaß	fun
Spiel	game
spielen	play
Spielzeug	toy
Sportzentrum	sports centre
sprechen	speak
sprechen (mit)	talk (to)
(über)springen	jump
Stadt	town
(Groß)Stadt	city
Stand	stall
stark	strong
stehen	stand
stellen	put
Strand	beach

Straße	road, street
Stuhl	chair
Stunde	hour
(Unterrichts)Stunde	lesson
Stundenplan	timetable
Sturm	storm
stürzen	fall
suchen nach	look for
Supermarkt	supermarket
süß	lovely
Süßigkeiten	sweets *(Mz)*

T

Tafel	board
Tag	day
Tante	aunt
tanzen	dance
Tasche	bag
Taschengeld	pocket money
Taschenrechner	calculator
Tasse	cup
Technik, Technologie	technology
Tee	tea
Telefon	telephone
Telefonkarte	phonecard
teuer	expensive
Tier	animal
Tiger	tiger
Tisch	table
Tischtennis	table tennis
Tochter	daughter
Toilette	toilet
Tomate	tomato (Mz: tomatoes)
Torte	cake
Tourist/in	tourist
tragen *(Kleidung)*	wear
träumen	dream
(sich) treffen, kennen lernen	meet
trinken	drink
trocken	dry
Tschüss!	bye
Tür	door

U

U-Bahn *(in London)*	tube
U-Bahn-Station	station
U-Bahn-Wagen	train
über	about, over
überqueren	cross
übrig	left
... Uhr	... o'clock
um (... Uhr)	at
Um wie viel Uhr?	What time?
um ... herum	around
umbringen	kill
umsonst	free

und	and
unfreundlich	unfriendly
ungefähr	about
ungewöhnlich	unusual
Uniform	uniform
uns	us
unser(e)	our
unten	down, at the bottom
unter	under
Unterrichtsstunde	lesson
unterwegs sein	be out
Urlaub	holiday

V

Vater	father
verbringen	spend
vergessen	forget
verkaufen	sell
verlassen	leave
verlieren	lose
Verlierer	loser
verschieden	different
versuchen	try
Verwandtschaft	family
viel	much
Viel Glück!	Good luck.
viel(e)	a lot of
viele	many
vielleicht	perhaps
Viertel (vor/nach)	quarter (to/past)
Vogel	bird
voll	full
von	from, of, about
vor	in front of *(örtlich)*, to *(Uhrzeit)*
vor (2 Minuten)	(2 minutes) ago
Vorführung	show
Vormittag	morning
vorsichtig, behutsam	careful

W

wahr	true
wann	when
warm	warm
warten	wait
warum	why
was	what
Was ist los?	What's the matter?
(sich) waschen	wash
Wasser	water
Wecker	alarm clock
Weg	way
weg, fort	away
weggehen	leave
weich	soft
Weihnachten	Christmas
weil	because

weiß	white
Welt	world
wenn	when
wer	who
werden *(Zukunft)*	will
nicht werden	won't (= will not)
Wetter	weather
Wettkampf, -spiel	match
wie	how
(so) wie	like
Wie bitte?	Sorry?
Wie ist ...?, Wie sieht ... aus?	What's ... like?
Wie ist/sind ...?	What is/are ... like?
Wie schade!	What a pity.
Wie viel kostet ...?	How much is ...?
Wie viel Uhr ist es?	What's the time?
wie viele?	how many?
Wie wäre es mit?, Was ist mit?	What about?
wieder	again
wild	wild
Wind	wind
Winter	winter
wir	we
wirklich	really
wissen	know
wo	where
Woche	week
Wochenende	weekend
wohnen	live
Wohnzimmer	living-room

Wolke	cloud
wollen	want
Wort	word
wunderbar	wonderful
wünschen	wish
Würstchen	sausage

Z

Zahl	number
zählen	count
Zeichen	sign
zeigen	show
Zeit	time
Zeitschrift	magazine
Zeitung	newspaper
Zelt	tent
ziehen	pull
ziemlich	quite
Zimmer	room
Zoo	zoo
(all)zu	too
zu Hause, daheim	at home
zu, nach, für	to
Zucker	sugar
Zug	train
zumachen	close
zurück	back
zusammen	together
zuschauen	watch
zweimal	twice
zwischen	between

Names

Girls/Women
Bina ['biːnə]
Brenda ['brendə]
Cauvery [kɔː'verɪ]
Chitra ['tʃɪtrə]
Claire [kleə]
Emma ['emə]
Firaki [fɪ'rɑːkɪ]
Gillian ['dʒɪljən]
Mary ['meərɪ]
Nasaar [nə'sɑː]
Pat [pæt]
Patsy ['pætsɪ]
Rhonda ['rɒndə]
Sheree [ʃɪ'riː]
Sue [suː]
Susan ['suːzn]
Terry ['terɪ]
Vera ['vɪərə]

Boys/Men
Chacko ['tʃʌkəʊ]
Charlie ['tʃɑːlɪ]
David ['deɪvɪd]
Eddy ['edɪ]
Geoff [dʒef]
Jack [dʒæk]
James [dʒeɪmz]
Karim [kʌ'riːm]
Mark [mɑːk]
Max [mæks]
Pete [piːt]
Pillai ['pɪlaɪ]
Pradeep [prə'diːp]
Robin ['rɒbɪn]
Roger ['rɒdʒə]
Tom [tɒm]
Victor ['vɪktə]
Wally ['wɒlɪ]
Yoyo ['jəʊjəʊ]

Families
Collins ['kɒlɪnz]
Conroy ['kɒnrɔɪ]
Dixon ['dɪksn]
Goodbody ['gʊdbɒdɪ]
Graham ['greɪəm]
Hartley ['hɑːtlɪ]
Khan [kɑːn]
Macintosh ['mækɪntɒʃ]
Mulloy [ˌmʌ'lɔɪ]
Pattison ['pætɪsn]
Ram [ræm]
Simpson ['sɪmpsn]

Smith [smɪθ]
Stopwhistle ['stɒpwɪsl]
Tan Fong [tæn 'fɒŋ]
Wilkins ['wɪlkɪnz]

Other Names
Beefeater ['biːfiːtə]
Belgravia ['belgreɪvɪə]
Birmingham ['bɜːmɪŋəm]
Boots [buːts]
Brighton ['braɪtn]
British Isles [ˌbrɪtɪʃ_'aɪlz]
Buckingham Palace [ˌbʌkɪŋəm 'pæləs]
Caernarfon Castle [kə,nɑːvən 'kɑːsl]
chapati [tʃə'pɑːtɪ]
Cologne [kə'ləʊn]
Cornwall ['kɔːnwɔːl]
Covent Garden [ˌkɒvənt 'gɑːdn]
Dark Crystal [ˌdɑːk 'krɪstl]
Diwali [dɪ'wɑːlɪ]
Dorset ['dɔːsɪt]
Durdle Door [ˌdɜːdl 'dɔː]
Ealing Town Hall [ˌiːlɪŋ 'taʊn hɔːl]
Flame [fleɪm]
Frankenstein ['fræŋkənstaɪn]
Geraldine ['dʒerəldiːn]
Guinness Book of Records [ˌgɪnɪs bʊk_əv 'rekɔːdz]
Hegira ['hedʒɪrə]
Hendon School [ˌhendən 'skuːl]
Highland Games ['haɪlənd geɪmz]
Hogmanay ['hɒgməneɪ]
Holland Park School ['hɒlənd pɑːk 'skuːl]
Hyde Park ['haɪd pɑːk]
Isle of Man [ˌaɪl_əv 'mæn]
Jack the Ripper [ˌdʒæk ðə 'rɪpə]
Jersey ['dʒɜːzɪ]
Jupiter ['dʒuːpɪtə]
Kensington Gardens [ˌkenzɪŋtən 'gɑːdnz]
Lakshmi ['lɑːkʃmɪ]
Little Red Riding Hood [ˌlɪtl red 'raɪdɪŋ hʊd]
Llanfair ... Railway Station [ˌlæn feə ... 'reɪlweɪ ˌsteɪʃn]
Loch Ness [lɒk 'nes]
London [ˌlʌndən]

London Toy and Model Museum [ˌlʌndən ˌtɔɪ_ən 'mɒdl mjuːˌzɪəm]
London Zoo [ˌlʌndən 'zuː]
Madame Tussaud's [mə,dɑːm tə'sɔːdz]
Madonna [mə'dɒnə]
Major Kira [ˌmeɪdʒə 'kɪərə]
Manhattan [mæn'hætn]
Marks & Spencer [ˌmɑːks_ən 'spensə]
Mars [mɑːz]
Mecca ['mekə]
Mickey Mouse ['mɪkɪ maʊs]
Mount McKinley [ˌmaʊnt mə'kɪnlɪ]
Mount Snowdon [maʊnt 'snəʊdn]
Muhammad [məʊ'hæmɪd]
National Park Service [ˌnæʃnl 'pɑːk ˌsɜːvɪs]
Natural History Museum [ˌnætʃrəl 'hɪstərɪ mjuːˌzɪəm]
North Pole [ˌnɔːθ 'pəʊl]
Notting Hill [ˌnɒtɪŋ 'hɪl]
Notting Hill News [ˌnɒtɪŋ hɪl 'njuːz]
Nottingham ['nɒtɪŋəm]
Old Shatterhand [ˌəʊld 'ʃætəhænd]
Oxford Circus [ˌɒksfəd 'sɜːkəs]
Oxford Street ['ɒksfəd ˌstriːt]
Piccadilly Circus [ˌpɪkədɪlɪ 'sɜːkəs]
Portobello Road [ˌpɔːtəʊˌbeləʊ 'rəʊd]
Prince [prɪns]
Radio Junior Europe [ˌreɪdɪəʊ ˌdʒuːnjə 'jʊərəp]
Rama ['rɑːmə]
Regent's Park [ˌriːdʒənts 'pɑːk]
Rhine [raɪn]
Robin Hood [ˌrɒbɪn 'hʊd]
Rockies ['rɒkɪz]
Rocky Mountains [ˌrɒkɪ 'maʊntɪnz]
Rolling Bones [ˌrəʊlɪŋ 'bəʊnz]
Round Pond [ˌraʊnd 'pɒnd]
Science Museum ['saɪəns mjuːˌzɪəm]
Segaworld ['siːgəˌwɜːld]
Selfridge ['selfrɪdʒ]
Sequoia National Park [sɪˌkwɔɪə næʃnl 'pɑːk]

Sheriff of Nottingham [ˌʃerɪf_əv ˈnɒtɪŋəm]
Sherwood Forest [ˌʃɜːwʊd ˈfɒrɪst]
Shetland Islands [ˌʃetlənd ˈaɪləndz]
Soho [ˈsəʊhəʊ]
Speakers' Corner [ˌspiːkəz ˈkɔːnə]
Statue of Liberty [ˌstætʃuː_əv ˈlɪbətɪ]
Sugar Boy [ˈʃʊgə bɔɪ]
Sunflower [ˈsʌnflaʊə]
Superman [ˈsuːpəmæn]
Superstore [ˈsuːpəstɔː]
Terry the tyrannosaurus [ˌterɪ ðə tɪˌrænəˈsɔːrəs]
Tower [ˈtaʊə]

Tower Bridge [ˈtaʊə brɪdʒ]
Urquhart Castle [ˌɜːkət ˈkɑːsl]
Vienna [vɪˈenə]
W.H.Smith's [ˌdʌblju: eɪtʃ ˈsmɪθs]
Woolworth's [ˈwʊlwəθs]
Yellowstone National Park [ˌjeləʊstəʊn næʃnl ˈpɑːk]
Yosemite National Park [jəʊˌsemɪtɪ næʃnl ˈpɑːk]
Yukon [ˈjuːkɒn]

Countries
Africa [ˈæfrɪkə]
Alaska [əˈlæskə]
America [əˈmerɪkə]
Asia [ˈeɪʃə]

Austria [ˈɔːstrɪə]
Britain [ˈbrɪtn]
Colorado [ˌkɒləˈrɑːdəʊ]
England [ˈɪŋglənd]
Germany [ˈdʒɜːmənɪ]
Great Britain [ˌgreɪt ˈbrɪtn]
Ireland [ˈaɪələnd]
Italy [ˈɪtəlɪ]
Mexico [ˈmeksɪkəʊ]
North America [ˌnɔːθ_əˈmerɪkə]
Scotland [ˈskɒtlənd]
South America [ˌsaʊθ_əˈmerɪkə]
Spain [speɪn]
Turkey [ˈtɜːkɪ]
USA [ˌjuː es ˈeɪ]
Wales [weɪlz]
Wyoming [ˌwaɪˈəʊmɪŋ]

Do it in English

In diesem Abschnitt findest du eine Sammlung von Sätzen und Ausdrücken, die dir helfen sollen, dich mit jemandem auf Englisch zu unterhalten. Du kannst sie auswendig lernen und dann mit deinem Partner / deiner Partnerin eigene Dialoge zusammenstellen und ausprobieren.

Theme 1

1 Ein Reiseziel erfragen: *Where did you go for your holiday?*
2 Nach dem Wetter fragen: *What was the weather like?*
3 Sagen, wie eine Sache / ein Ereignis war: *It was great / not bad / terrible.*
4 Fragen, was jemand getan hat: *What did you do?*
5 Einen Brief an einen Freund / eine Freundin beginnen: *Dear Pete,*
         Thanks a million for ...
         I'm back at school after ...
6 Einen Brief, eine Postkarte beenden: *Love, Brenda*
         See you soon, Pete
         Bye for now, Mary
7 Fragen/sagen, wie viel Uhr es ist: *What's the time?*
         It's quarter past nine.
         It's half past six.
         It's quarter to eleven.
8 Jemanden loben: *Well done, Patsy.*

Theme 2

1 Erleichterung ausdrücken: *Oh, thank goodness.*
2 Sich entschuldigen, dass man zu spät kommt: *Sorry we're late.*
3 Einen Vorschlag machen: *Why don't we all go to the zoo?*
         Let's take the tube.
4 Sagen, was man tun möchte: *I want to see the elephants.*
5 Gründe angeben: *I think it's interesting.*
         I want to see the chimpanzees because they are funny.
6 Sagen, dass man/jemand Angst hat(te):   *I was so frightened.*
         Gillian is very frightened.

Theme 3

1 Eine Vorhersage machen: *David will be a cowboy.*
         Or perhaps he'll be an astronaut.
2 Sagen, dass jemand vorsichtig sein soll: *Be careful!*
3 Einen Wettlauf starten/beenden: *Ready, steady, go!*
         Stop! Time's up!
4 Sagen, was man/jemand gut / nicht so gut kann: *She's very good at science.*
         He's not so good at sports.
5 Sagen, dass jemand gut aussieht: *She looks beautiful.*
6 Jemandem Glück wünschen: *Good luck!*

Do it in English

Theme 4

1 Sagen, was man/jemand vorhat:

2 Jemandem ein gutes neues Jahr wünschen:
3 Etwas vergleichen:

4 Sagen, dass man/jemand etwas nicht tun braucht:
5 Etwas bedauern:

I'm going to put the presents on the table.
Mr Williams is going to phone the police.
Happy New Year!

The red scarf is cheaper than the green scarf.
The perfume is as expensive as the handbag.
Your cake is the loveliest cake of all.
You needn't bring anything.

What a pity I only have one birthday a year.

Theme 5

1 Sagen, dass man/jemand etwas tun muss:

2 Sagen, dass man/jemand etwas nicht tun darf:
3 Fragen, ob jemand etwas darf:

4 Seine Meinung zu etwas äußern:

5 Sagen, was wichtig ist:
6 Einen Vorschlag machen:

I have to do my homework before I can go out.
Pupils must be polite.
Gillian mustn't watch TV after 9 o'clock.

Can you stay up late?
Can you go to discos?
I think it's more expensive to wear jeans and sweatshirts to school.
I'm for/against school uniforms.
It's very important to look at the traffic signs.
What about a track just for bikers?

Theme 6

1 Jemanden auf später vertrösten:
2 Fragen ob / sagen, dass jemand schon etwas getan hat:
3 Fragen/sagen, wofür man/jemand sich interessiert:
4 Sagen, was man/jemand sehr gern tun möchte:
5 Sagen, dass sich jemand beruhigen soll:

In a minute.
Have you ever visited the Rockies before?
David has read a book about castles.
What are you interested in?
Lisa is interested in horses.
Charlie would love to buy a present for Lisa.
I'd love to fly in a helicopter.
Don't worry.
Cool down.

Classroom phrases

Wenn man ankommt oder geht

Good morning.	Guten Morgen.
Sorry, I'm late.	Tut mir leid, dass ich zu spät komme.
Sorry, I don't have my exercise book with me.	Tut mir leid, ich habe mein Heft nicht dabei.
Sorry, I don't have my homework with me.	Tut mir leid, ich habe meine Hausaufgaben nicht dabei.
What's for homework?	Was haben wir als Hausaufgabe auf?
See you tomorrow.	Bis morgen.
Bye-bye.	Tschüs.

Wenn es ein Problem gibt

What's the matter with you?	Was ist mit dir los?
I'm fine.	Mir geht's gut.
I feel sick.	Mir ist schlecht.
I have a headache.	Ich habe Kopfschmerzen.
Can I open the window, please?	Kann ich bitte das Fenster öffnen?
Can I go to the toilet, please?	Kann ich bitte zur Toilette gehen?

Wenn man Hilfe braucht

Can you help me, please?	Können Sie / Kannst du mir bitte helfen?
I have a question.	Ich habe eine Frage.
I don't understand this.	Ich verstehe das hier nicht.
How can I do this exercise?	Wie mache ich diese Aufgabe?
What's … in English/German?	Was heißt … auf Englisch/Deutsch?
What does … mean?	Was bedeutet …?
Can you write it on the board, please?	Können Sie / Kannst du das bitte an die Tafel schreiben?
Can you say that again, please?	Können Sie / Kannst du das bitte noch einmal sagen?
Sorry, I don't know.	Tut mir leid, das weiß ich nicht.
What page, please?	Auf welcher Seite bitte?

Wenn man zusammen arbeitet oder spielt

Whose turn is it?	Wer ist dran?
I like (don't like) this story.	Diese Geschichte gefällt mir (nicht).
I think it's good/interesting/funny.	Ich finde sie gut/interessant/komisch.
I think it's terrible/boring/sad.	Ich finde sie schrecklich/langweilig/traurig.
Can I be …?	Kann ich … sein/spielen?
Do you want to work with me?	Möchtest du mit mir arbeiten?

Was der Lehrer / die Lehrerin sagt

Open your books at page …
Turn to page …
Look at line …
Read the text on page …

Öffnet eure Bücher auf Seite …
Blättert zu Seite …
Seht euch Zeile … an.
Lest den Text auf Seite …

Work in pairs.
Work in teams of four.
Sit in a circle.

Arbeitet zu zweit.
Arbeitet zu viert.
Bildet einen Sitzkreis.

Listen to the CD.
Write about …
Talk about …
Ask questions about …
Answer the question, please.
Match the sentences.
Who wants to read the text?
Write the answers down.

Hör/Hört die CD an.
Schreibe/Schreibt über …
Sprich/Sprecht über …
Stelle/Stellt Fragen zu …
Beantworte/Beantwortet bitte die Frage.
Ordne/Ordnet die Sätze zu.
Wer möchte den Text vorlesen?
Schreibt die Antworten auf.

Act it.
Change roles.
Make your own dialogue.
Take a card.

Spiel/Spielt es vor.
Tauscht die Rollen.
Entwirf/Entwerft selbst ein Gespräch.
Nimm/Nehmt eine Karte.

Come to the board, please.
Collect the exercise books, please.
Do this exercise at home, please.

Komm/Kommt bitte zur Tafel.
Sammelt bitte die Hefte ein.
Macht diese Aufgabe bitte zu Hause.

Be quiet.
Sit down.
Please speak up.

Sei/Seid ruhig.
Setz dich. / Setzt euch.
Sprich bitte lauter.

You can do better.
Try again.
That's it.
Well done.

Das kannst du besser.
Versuch es noch einmal.
Das ist alles.
Gut gemacht.

Unregelmäßige Verben

infinitive	simple past	
be [biː]	was/were [wɒz/wɜː]	sein
bring [brɪŋ]	brought [brɔːt]	(mit)bringen
buy [baɪ]	bought [bɔːt]	kaufen
can [kæn]	could [kʊd]	können
catch [kætʃ]	caught [kɔːt]	fangen
come [kʌm]	came [keɪm]	kommen
do [duː]	did [dɪd]	machen, tun
drink [drɪŋk]	drank [dræŋk]	trinken
eat [iːt]	ate [eɪt]	essen, fressen
fall [fɔːl]	fell [fel]	fallen, stürzen
feed [fiːd]	fed [fed]	füttern
fight [faɪt]	fought [fɔːt]	kämpfen
find [faɪnd]	found [faʊnd]	finden
fly [flaɪ]	flew [fluː]	fliegen
forget [fəˈget]	forgot [fəˈgɒt]	vergessen
get [get]	got [gɒt]	bekommen; gelangen
give [gɪv]	gave [geɪv]	geben
go [gəʊ]	went [went]	gehen
have [hæv]	had [hæd]	haben
hear [hɪə]	heard [hɜːd]	hören
keep [kiːp]	kept [kept]	behalten, halten
know [nəʊ]	knew [njuː]	wissen, kennen
leave [liːv]	left [left]	verlassen, weggehen
lie [laɪ]	lay [leɪ]	liegen
lose [luːz]	lost [lɒst]	verlieren
make [meɪk]	made [meɪd]	machen, tun
meet [miːt]	met [met]	(sich) treffen, kennen lernen
put [pʊt]	put [pʊt]	legen, setzen, stellen
read [riːd]	read [red]	lesen
ride [raɪd]	rode [rəʊd]	reiten, fahren
run [rʌn]	ran [ræn]	rennen, laufen
say [seɪ]	said [sed]	sagen
see [siː]	saw [sɔː]	sehen
sell [sel]	sold [səʊld]	verkaufen
send [send]	sent [sent]	senden, schicken
sing [sɪŋ]	sang [sæŋ]	singen
sit [sɪt]	sat [sæt]	sitzen, sich setzen
sleep [sliːp]	slept [slept]	schlafen
smell [smel]	smelt [smelt]	riechen, duften, stinken
speak [spiːk]	spoke [spəʊk]	sprechen
spend [spend]	spent [spent]	verbringen
stand [stænd]	stood [stʊd]	stehen
swim [swɪm]	swam [swæm]	schwimmen
take [teɪk]	took [tʊk]	nehmen, bringen
tell [tel]	told [təʊld]	sagen, erzählen
think [θɪŋk]	thought [θɔːt]	denken, glauben, meinen
wear [weə]	wore [wɔː]	tragen (Kleidung)
win [wɪn]	won [wʌn]	gewinnen
write [raɪt]	wrote [rəʊt]	schreiben

The date

we write:			we say:
1st April	or	**1 April**	the first of April
2nd May	or	**2 May**	the second of May
3rd June	or	**3 June**	the third of June
4th July	or	**4 July**	the forth of July

Months

January ['dʒænjʊərɪ]	Januar
February ['februərɪ]	Februar
March [mɑːtʃ]	März
April ['eɪprl]	April
May [meɪ]	Mai
June [dʒuːn]	Juni
July [dʒʊ'laɪ]	Juli
August ['ɔːgəst]	August
September [sep'tembə]	September
October [ɒk'təʊbə]	Oktober
November [nəʊ'vembə]	November
December [dɪ'sembə]	Dezember

Numbers

1	one [wʌn]	11	eleven [ɪ'levn]	21	twenty-one [ˌtwenti 'wʌn]
2	two [tuː]	12	twelve [twelv]	...	
3	three [θriː]	13	thirteen [ˌθɜː'tiːn]	30	thirty ['θɜːtɪ]
4	four [fɔː]	14	fourteen [ˌfɔː'tiːn]	40	forty ['fɔːtɪ]
5	five [faɪv]	15	fifteen [ˌfɪf'tiːn]	50	fifty ['fɪftɪ]
6	six [sɪks]	16	sixteen [ˌsɪks'tiːn]	60	sixty ['sɪkstɪ]
7	seven ['sevn]	17	seventeen [ˌsevn'tiːn]	70	seventy ['sevntɪ]
8	eight [eɪt]	18	eighteen [ˌeɪ'tiːn]	80	eighty ['eɪtɪ]
9	nine [naɪn]	19	nineteen [ˌnaɪn'tiːn]	90	ninety ['naɪntɪ]
10	ten [ten]	20	twenty ['twentɪ]	100	one hundred [wʌn 'hʌndrəd]

Ordinal Numbers

1st	**first** [fɜːst]	11th	eleventh [ɪ'levnθ]	21st	twenty-**first** [ˌtwentɪ'fɜːst]
2nd	**second** ['sekənd]	12th	twel**fth** [twelfθ]	22nd	twenty-**second** [ˌtwentɪ'sekənd]
3rd	**third** [θɜːd]	13th	thirteenth [ˌθɜː'tiːnθ]	23rd	twenty-**third** [ˌtwentɪ'θɜːd]
4th	fourth [fɔːθ]	14th	fourteenth [ˌfɔː'tiːnθ]	24th	twenty-**fourth** [ˌtwentɪ'fɔːθ]
5th	fi**fth** [fɪfθ]	15th	fifteenth [ˌfɪf'tiːnθ]	25th	twenty-fifth [ˌtwentɪ'fɪfθ]
6th	sixth [sɪksθ]	16th	sixteenth [ˌsɪks'tiːnθ]	26th	twenty-sixth [ˌtwentɪ'sɪksθ]
7th	seventh ['sevnθ]	17th	seventeenth [ˌsevn'tiːnθ]	27th	twenty-seventh [ˌtwentɪ'sevnθ]
8th	eighth [eɪtθ]	18th	eighteenth [ˌeɪ'tiːnθ]	28th	twenty-eighth [ˌtwentɪ'eɪtθ]
9th	ni**nth** [naɪnθ]	19th	nineteenth [ˌnaɪn'tiːnθ]	29th	twenty-ninth [ˌtwentɪ'naɪnθ]
10th	tenth [tenθ]	20th	twent**ieth** ['twentɪəθ]	30th	thirt**ieth** ['θɜːtɪəθ]
				31st	thirty-first [ˌθɜːtɪ'fɜːst]

Bildquellen:

Umschlag außen: Tony Stone / D. Reese, Hamburg (großes Titelfoto); Tony Stone / G. Allison, Hamburg (kl. Foto vorn); Tony Stone / D. Madison, Hamburg (kl. Foto hinten)

Innenumschlag vorn: Dr. Peter Güttler, Berlin (Karte London)

11 Bavaria/Nägele, München (Mount Snowdon)

12 dpa/Brakemeier, Frankfurt/M. (Snowdon Mountain Railway)

13 Bavaria/Nägele, München (Mount Snowdon)

14/15 British Tourist Authority, London (Llanfair…); Bavaria / W. Meier, München (Durdle Door); British Tourist Authority, London (Highland Games); Bavaria / D. Ball, München (Urquhart Castle)

16/17 British Tourist Authority, London (The Argyllshire Gathering, Strathclyde)

18 Manhattan Post Card Pub. Co. Inc. / J. Lantero, Glendale, N.Y.; Verlag Bauer / H. Popelka, Wien (Stephansdom); Verlag D. Grimmer / E. Braun, Tübingen (Burg Hohenzollern); Karan & Simpson, Bodrum, Türkei

22 Bavaria, München (Burg Rheinstein)

24 Gisela Schultz-Steinbach (Postkasten)

26 Reinhard Jonczyk (Sekretariat); Claudia Straeter-Lietz (Lehrer)

27 Bavaria, München (Tiger); Thomas Kern (Polizisten)

28 Bavaria, München (Tiger)

29 MEV Verlag GmbH, Augsburg (Elefant)

31 Silvestris/Lane, Kastle (Delfin); ZEFA, Düsseldorf (Delfin)

33 Thomas Kern (Polizisten)

34 Tony Stone / Rowan, München (Krokodil); ZEFA/Horus, Düsseldorf (Eisbären); MEV Verlag GmbH, Augsburg (Elefant); ZEFA/Hanusch, Düsseldorf (Schimpanse); Bavaria, München (Flamingos)

35 Bavaria/Lewis, München (Löwe); Tony Stone / Rowan, München (Nilpferd, Seelöwen); Bavaria, München (Tiger)

36 Joe Wright, UK (Hunde); Inga Moore, UK (Giraffe)

37 London Zoo, London (Logo, Lageplan)

38/39 Dr. Peter Güttler, Berlin (Karte)

40/41 ZEFA, UK (Tower Bridge)

40 Transglobe/Richardson, Hamburg (Trafalgar Square); Gordon Cardno (Jongleur); Look / Chr. Heeb, München (Hyde Park); Schweitzer, München (Buckingham Palace)

41 Bavaria/Scholz, München (10 Downing Street); ZEFA/Damm, Düsseldorf (Big Ben); Bavaria, München (City Skyline)

42 ZEFA/Smith, Düsseldorf (Beefeater); dpa/Leuschner, Frankfurt/M. (Krone); Bavaria, München (Tower)

43 Dr. Peter Güttler, Berlin (Karte)

44 Reinhard Jonczyk (Schüler)

45 dpa, Frankfurt/M. (Old Shatterhand, Robin Hood, Superman)

47 dpa, Frankfurt/M. (Robin Hood)

48 dpa, Frankfurt/M. (Superman, Old Shatterhand); Cinetext, Frankfurt/M. (Major Kira Nerys)

52 Painter 4.0 © 1994 Photo Disc (Stoppuhr)

57 Reinhard Jonczyk (Instrumente)

58 Schuster/Tovy, Oberursel (Musikanten)

59 Thomas Kern (Einkaufsstraße)

60 Bavaria / W. Rauch, München (Feuerwerk)

61 Reinhard Jonczyk (Projektarbeit)

62 dpa, Frankfurt/M. (Diwali, Bombay); Henriette Vahle (Chapati)

63 Bavaria/Viesti, München (Diwali, Katmandu)

64/65 LINK Picture Library / O. Eliason, London (Indian store)

66 Schapowalow/Lokie, Hamburg (Drachentanz); British Tourist Authority, London (First Footing, Scotland)

68 MAURITIUS/Vidler, Mittenwald (Oxford Street)

74 Thomas Kern (Einkaufsstraße)

75 Christoph Edelhoff (Mädchen)

76 MEV Verlag GmbH, Augsburg (Zettel)

77 Henriette Vahle (Ohrringe)

78 Stock Photography auf Photoshop 4.0 OS 14120, Adobe Systems Inc. (Medaille)

79 Bavaria, München (Moskito, Blauwal, Läuferinnen)

80 Gisela Schultz-Steinbach (Plakat)

81 Christoph Edelhoff (Mädchen); Gordon Cardno (Junge); Claudia Straeter-Lietz (Schulklasse)

83 Antony Radburn, UK (Radfahrer)

84 Bavaria/Vega, München (Tokio); Christoph Edelhoff (London); Bronwyn Grieve (Look right)

86 Katharine Eastham (Fahrrad); Bavaria, München (Jungen)

Textquellen:

87 Bavaria, München (Grizzlybären)
89 Bavaria, München (Rocky Mountain NP, Kojote)
90 Bavaria, München (Grizzlybären); Bavaria / S. Wind, München (Geysir)
91 Bavaria / H.R. Bramaz, München (Tyrannosaurus Rex)
92 Tony Stone, London (Tischtennis); Topham Picturepoint, Edenbridge (Pferd); MEV Verlag GmbH, Augsburg (Ballon)
95 Claudia Straeter-Lietz (Schüler)
96 Bavaria, München (Tiger)
Innenumschlag hinten: Dr. Peter Güttler, Berlin (Karte UK)

25 Ellis, Printha: "The school chant", © Schroedel Verlag GmbH, Hannover
50 Hoberman, Mary Ann: "Tiger", © Mary Ann Hoberman; Kitching, John: "My name is Supermouse", "Dogs", © John Kitching; West, Colin: "Geraldine Giraffe", © Colin West.

Nicht alle Copyrightinhaber konnten ermittelt werden; deren Urheberrechte werden hiermit vorsorglich anerkannt.

Grammar glossary:

Adjektiv	adjective ['ædʒɪktɪv]	beautiful, dark, fast, …
Artikel	article ['ɑːtɪkl]	
(bestimmter)	(definite) ['defnɪt]	the
(unbestimmter)	(indefinite) [ɪn'defnɪt]	a, an
Einzahl (Singular)	singular ['sɪŋgjələ]	child, house, pen, …
Frage	question ['kwestʃən]	How old are you?
Gegenwart (Präsens)	present tense [ˌpreznt 'tens]	
(einfache Form)	simple present [ˌsɪmpl 'preznt]	She plays football. She doesn't play tennis.
(Verlaufsform)	present progressive [ˌpreznt prəʊ'gresɪv]	He's lying in the sun. He isn't swimming.
Mehrzahl (Plural)	plural ['plʊərəl]	children, houses, pens, …
Nomen	noun [naʊn]	bike, girl, weather, …
Präposition	preposition [ˌprepə'zɪʃn]	in, behind, next to, …
Pronomen	pronoun ['prəʊnaʊn]	I, you, he, she, … / my, your, his, her, … / me, you, him, her, …
Satz	sentence ['sentəns]	My name is Susan.
Verb	verb [vɜːb]	catch, read, swim, …
Vergangenheit	past tense [ˌpɑːst 'tens]	
(einfache Form)	simple past [ˌsɪmpl 'pɑːst]	She visited some friends. She didn't stay at home.
Vergleich	comparison [kəm'pærɪsən]	The cap is cheaper than the scarf. / The teddy is more expensive than the dinosaur. The blue shoes are as nice as the black shoes.
Vollendete Gegenwart (Perfekt)	present perfect [ˌpreznt 'pɜːfɪkt]	She has caught a cold. I've talked to her before.
Wortstellung	word order ['wɜːd ˌɔːdə]	
Zukunft (Futur)	future ['fjuːtʃə]	I will help you. He is going to buy a pet.

Diesterweg

Bestellkarte   Hiermit bestelle ich   (einfach ankreuzen)

Begleitmaterial zu **Portobello Road 2**   D 71502

☐   **Workbook 2**
    Arbeitsheft zum Schülerbuch
    80 S. mit zahlreichen Abbildungen
    ISBN 3-507-**71512**-0   DM 10,90

☐   **Kassette 2**   (Inhalt identisch mit CD)
    Begleitkassette zum Schülerbuch und Arbeitsheft
    mit Texten, Liedern und Übungen
    Laufzeit ca. 75 Min.
    ISBN 3-507-**71532**-5   DM 29,90*

☐   **CD 2**   (Inhalt identisch mit Kassette)
    Begleit-CD zum Schülerbuch und Arbeitsheft
    mit Texten, Liedern und Übungen
    Laufzeit ca. 75 Min.
    ISBN 3-507-**71562**-7   DM 29,90*

Alle Titel sind auch über den Buchhandel erhältlich.
Preisstand 1.1.1999. Änderungen vorbehalten. * Unverbindliche Preisempfehlung.
Die Lieferung erfolgt auf Rechnung (Preis zuzüglich Versandkosten).

Bestellkarte   Hiermit bestelle ich   (einfach ankreuzen)

Begleitmaterial zu **Portobello Road 2**   D 71502

☐   **Workbook 2**
    Arbeitsheft zum Schülerbuch
    80 S. mit zahlreichen Abbildungen
    ISBN 3-507-**71512**-0   DM 10,90

☐   **Kassette 2**   (Inhalt identisch mit CD)
    Begleitkassette zum Schülerbuch und Arbeitsheft
    mit Texten, Liedern und Übungen
    Laufzeit ca. 75 Min.
    ISBN 3-507-**71532**-5   DM 29,90*

☐   **CD 2**   (Inhalt identisch mit Kassette)
    Begleit-CD zum Schülerbuch und Arbeitsheft
    mit Texten, Liedern und Übungen
    Laufzeit ca. 75 Min.
    ISBN 3-507-**71562**-7   DM 29,90*

Alle Titel sind auch über den Buchhandel erhältlich.
Preisstand 1.1.1999. Änderungen vorbehalten. * Unverbindliche Preisempfehlung.
Die Lieferung erfolgt auf Rechnung (Preis zuzüglich Versandkosten).

Diesterweg

Bitte in Druckschrift ausfüllen

Vorname

Name

Straße / Hausnummer

Postleitzahl / Ort

Datum / Unterschrift
(bei Minderjährigen Unterschrift der/des Erziehungsberechtigten)

Bitte
frankieren

Antwortkarte

**Verlag
Moritz Diesterweg**

D-30517 Hannover

Ich bin damit einverstanden, dass meine
Daten elektronisch gespeichert werden.

Bitte in Druckschrift ausfüllen

Vorname

Name

Straße / Hausnummer

Postleitzahl / Ort

Datum / Unterschrift
(bei Minderjährigen Unterschrift der/des Erziehungsberechtigten)

Bitte
frankieren

Antwortkarte

**Verlag
Moritz Diesterweg**

D-30517 Hannover

Ich bin damit einverstanden, dass meine
Daten elektronisch gespeichert werden.